Anataalie's Psychic Duels

Anataalie's vanilla and blueberry trail

MALOVEL Series—Part I of X

Anataalie's Psychic Duels

Dazzling trails of Malovel

Rahman, Brigitte Arlette

Writers Club Press
San Jose New York Lincoln Shanghai

Anataalie's Psychic Duels
Dazzling trails of Malovel

Writers Club Press
an imprint of iUniverse, Inc.

For information address:
iUniverse, Inc.
5220 S. 16th St., Suite 200
Lincoln, NE 68512
www.iuniverse.com

ISBN: 0-595-20480-5

Printed in the United States of America

EPIGRAPH

ERASE MY GRAVE

In the land of autumn,the wind axes away
the violins in La chanson d'Automne
and clear the way to a new day

Rusted sonnets had sealed the vault
where the drums and the scriptures
Still fight about their last page in history.

Blow hard and strong, wind
please destroy for me
that monument to absurdity
erase my name, erase my grave
While time is still ticking painfully…

Open the black bellies of the cemeteries
and let the prayer of my souls fly free

Blow that hasty kiss
To my last day decimated in counted moments.
I did never asked to be
Now I do ask to be no more.
but that autumn leaf that you keep floating
in that last season of your heart
Rahman, brigitte arlette-Series Malovel-

CONTENTS

FOREWORD

it is hard to shake your hand

A rug in Afghanistan
whispers the tale of an old man
maimed by a land mine
weaving the love fibers
into a pattern exquisite of a soulful warmth
pearling from his atrophied fingers

A sculpture in Greece
breathes in the marble of the intellect
a classical sigh
Eros has been mutilated so often
by the sword of the impossible love

A farmer on an Iraqi field,
recites the truth of his prayers, and
heals the land with his sweat
as a new born dies once more
never far away from his tears

It is hard to shake your hand
it is hard to receive a hug
my heart has been broken so often
By your unconditional love.

Rahman,brigitte arlette-Series Rehlati-

PREFACE

Chains of Passion

As I watch over you
parading once again an act
meant to inflate each of your words
I am left with no choice.
but to let the false praises
fly gently in the summer breeze

With the sting of the voodoo needle
I burst open the sorry balloons.

From the wrecks in the air
a healing storm of musical notes
releases, in my heart, Mozart
and Jaisini
from the chains of passion
And devotion.
And so I know that our song
shall be sung for all
And it will be heard by all.

Rahman,brigitte arlette-Series Jours Blancs

Mystical Short Stories and Poetry
Poetry
Rahman, Brigitte Arlette

Short Story 1

The Madness of the Sufi Poet

At a poetry soiree, Abdul-Wahab had been invited in Paris to be the chief guest of honor by Mme Blanchet.

Mme Blanchet was a semi-mundane, and a musician, she loved displaying her music skills to her bourgeois friends, and entertain others. Her invitations were always accepted with anticipation. She was a generous lady and was known to have a certain wealth. None knew her well, but no questions were raised either.

Her mansion was exquisitely decorated with antiques, and chandeliers, Persian carpets, sculptures, her verandah was the favorite part, and in summer evenings, iron wrought tables made in Provence were set there in a stage like arrangement. Her garden was legendary, it was an orchard, and in the summer nights the fruity scents were both stimulating and soothing. There was too her incredible green house where she kept several kinds of orchids…she did not like flowers very much, she did not like those with thorns, or those that were used to decorate tombs at the graveyards….

Yes everyone in different part of France and other countries always gleefully opened her letters, and when there was an invitation card, they smiled broadly. After all who could have forgotten the soiree of last year, when her daughter did get engaged to the son of a famous lawyer?

It had been an extravagant soiree, and she had spared no efforts to make it a success, She had engaged an orchestra and singers who sang the songs of La Rive Gauche, Edith Piaf, Mistinguet, and Maurice Chevalier. Everyone had dressed up nicely, put on long gowns and wore exquisite hats, the men were attired in tuxedos too. The front of the mansion was lined up with expensive cars from her limousine to the corvette of her son, to the Mercedes of her guests.

The party had been a delightful event, but the climax of that party, everyone remembered it well: and that was still the topic of many conversations. The maids had brought in the desert, the masterpiece of the French meal. It was a tall sculpture of petits choux, light pastry filled with a snow-white vanilla cream, iced with a perfect coat of orange flower almond paste.

Madame Blanchet had then stood up and said:

"Well, my good friends, in honor of my beautiful daughter, Anataalie, I shall personally serve each of you your desert."

And so she raised herself and went to the side trolley, and as the maid handed over each guest's desert plate, she carefully placed one petit choux at the center of the dish.

They all waited, as per French courtesy, that she had regained her seat at the table to resume the meal. She smiled and said:

"Warning for those of you who may not know, this is the masterpiece of this soiree, eat and chew before swallowing, chew three times."

She said loudly:

"I repeat, chew three times before you swallow."

They thought she was playing one of her games, or maybe she was a little inebriated from the joy of seeing the happiness on her daughter's face. But they were all gentlepeople, they said:

"Yes, Madame, of course…"

As they started to eat the desert, each of them chewed and soon each face became perplexed, each guest took their serviette/napkin and proceeded to remove a hardness they had found in the cream, and soon each one gave a delightful shriek or laugh: in each petit choux, there was a solitaire diamond, they were twenty-eight guests…

She had planted twenty-eight solitaire diamonds in the piece montee de petits-choux.

Guests were shocked…and wanted to thank her, but she evaded the thanks with a smile.

She laughed and said:

" Now: to my lovely Anataalie, here is the necklace that my mother gave me"

She opened a crimson ecrin, and an incredible sparkle came out of there: everyone gasped as she took it out, it was a river of diamonds 280 solitaires…a fortune by any standard.

That party was talked about it for years.

Today, again, Mrs.Blanchet's mansion was the venue of a soiree. She had mentioned that it would be a poetic soiree as she had invited an old friend from Mesopotamia: a famed Sufi poet Al Wahab.

Everyone was eager to reach on time; the place was so deliciously relaxing and full of anticipation. As usual everything was perfect, petits fours topped with caviar and violet petals glazed with pink sugar were served to the guests.

The anti-chambre was full with the most elegant people of Paris and other capitals of the world; an orchestra from Egypt was playing songs of Arabia in the honor of that distinguished Poet that had been crowned the Prince of Poetry in many cities of the world. It was rumored that he had been nominated to be one of the recipients of the next Nobel Prize for literature.

He was a man of sixty years, wearing a suit, impeccably groomed; he was with a walking stick of rosewood with a handle of pure silver. There was a look of a faded Rudolph Valentino in him, somehow, that was appealing.

Anaatalie had come too with her husband, and she was magnificent, she wore an embroidered dress of Arabia, and everyone stared at her in amazement: she was Sheherazade reincarnated.

Soon, Mrs.Blanchet clapped her hands and said:

"Silence everyone. Take your seat, and let us enjoy the poetry that our distinguished Poet will speak out to you from his heart to your heart."

The Egyptian orchestra stopped and the stage manager signed them over to play the next melody, it was a gentle Arabian melody based on three instruments the flute, the canoon and the ood…

Al Wahab stood in the middle of the podium and started reciting his poetry. It was magical, from the prison rhymes he had written when he had been captured and jailed for his beliefs to the softer poems of love, the flow went uninterrupted. Everyone was under his spell…. None spoke; his fiery stare and gentle voice hypnotized everyone: His words echoed deep in the guests' souls:

The white dove in my heart refuses to eat
I tried to feed her sweet words and serenades
But she will not eat. The wailing of her anguish
Maddens my days and nights…

Some strange noise came from the background, like a sob. . None really looked as everyone was enthralled by the poetry.

Soon everything was over, and the Egyptian orchestra proceeded to play a more dynamic music and Mona Ayyed, the most famous belly dancer of Egypt, was dancing on a mesmerizing tune. She was quite a sight too, and everyone was too hypnotized by her dance. It was so vibrant, so oriental

The soiree was another success. Mrs.Blanchet and her son in law were engaging the guests into conversations, gleaming with pride.

Everyone was there, except Abdul-Wahab and Anataalie who were in the green house…Anataalie was sitting near an orchid, crying gently

She heard some footstep coming closer as she looked up, Abdul-Wahab said:

"I am so sorry Anataalie, I should not have recited those verses.".

She said:

"Yes, you should not have, those were the verses you last wrote to me."

He sighed:

"Yes, I could not help it."

She said:

"Have you got your reply?"

He said:

"I look for no reply, I am a Sufi I have no expectations."

She asked:

"Has she died? "

The poet paused:

"She is dying, yes, she tries to do so but she cannot die and you know why?"

He pleaded:

"Please let her die, I am a prisoner of your heart, free me…You have captured my soul and as long as the white dove is alive, I am tortured. Let go of me, Anataalie. All my life is in vain, cannot you understand?"

She said:

"No."

And they both looked back on their lives and remembered how they had met the first time. Mrs.Blanchet had rented a villa for the summer in Madrid, and Abdul Wahad was occupying the villa next to theirs, he was a cultural attache of some embassy. They used to meet. She was then hardly fifteen and he had fallen madly in love with her. It was so easy to do, she was so very beautiful, many did fall in love with her, and she was used to it. But he was different, he was so unique, and that she understood.

He came and said to her one day:

"You know, I had a Sufi land in my soul until you, and none and nothing could tie me to life or death."

He repeated this over and over, but it was too late, he had fallen for her. She said nothing.

And he would pursue her, bring gifts and poems and wait for her, but she always said no. He had felt so much pain.

Once his friends said
"Abdul Wahab let us go to a nightclub."
He said:
"Yes, my soul has got to be tested"

They laughed they said
"Spanish women are something else, you know."
He said:
" I really do not care, let us go and we shall see. My soul cannot be possessed by a woman, anyway."

As he said this he felt a sharp stab in his heart, he heard Anataalie's soft voice in his captive soul.

They went and sat at a table close to the stage. It was a great place, everyone seemed to enjoy himself or herself so well, but he was bored, the stage program was boring, women were too insipid for his refined taste.

Suddenly something struck him hard, there she was on the stage, she wore a wig, had put make up but it was her!!..... And he became mad: he shouted aloud:

" Anataalie"

It was she, she run from the stage and disappeared into the night…

He went home and cried all night: he had wanted to give her respect and gentle love, why was she doing this there? How? He did not understand, he was mad with grief and disbelief.

In the early hours of that morning, he heard a knock and she was at the door. He said:

"Anataalie, go, please, I cannot see you."

She said.
"Yes"
He said:
"Yes what Anataalie?"
She said.
"Yes, tonight yes."
He felt his heart breaking, his soul ripped open as he cried:

"Can you not understand Anataalie, we are finished before we even started, and I could never love you now. Never. Go away."

The next day, he left and mailed her one poem:
I just cannot find the words to tell you this.
But yes perhaps the incantation formed
In the crater of my heart is the white dove within

I cannot tell her what to do, she is pure
She had been made to sing bliss
Then strangled by a tyrannical hand that
Needed to control the flow of her life

The white dove in my heart refuses to eat
I tried to feed her sweet words and serenades

But she will not eat. The wailing of her anguish
Maddens my days and nights

She trusted for the first time
She came to nestle in your hand,
You closed your fist on her to capture and torture her.

Yes I think I did find the words to tell you
Let her be, she does not have long to live
And what if she remembered a few of your lies?
Let her be, she is dying a painful death
She will never come to you again…

He sent her that poem…. And they never met again till now.

Today was one day after some ten years, and he had been haunted by her ever since. He had not long to live; he wanted to be free of her, to go to the Sufi Land of the Soul…. That is why he had come to Mrs.Blanchet soiree, for that sole purpose. To regain his freedom, to feel and feed on the disgust of that fatal night and be finally free from her.

But as he looked upon her loveliness in the green house, he knew that he would forever be a earthbound spirit, and that his poems would be the poems of eternity, that he would be put next to Shakespeare, as his soul in pain would never rest, ever.

He left the next day, and soon the news came that he had died in a plane crash, his body was never found.

-The end-

SHORT STORY 2

The Girls of Paper

One photograph was lying on the coffee table besides the old man 's armchair. He was living in Hungary, not so far away from civilization, but his house was an old habitat, eaten up by moisture and decay.

It was a two-room house, the way. Houses were made so long ago, one room downstairs and another of the same size up to which one could climb up to .by taking the steep stairs.

The door had no locks, no latch. And once, inside the lack of lock spoke of emptiness and want and void. The floor once tiled. had holes that had been filled with plaster, grayish plaster. There was no furnishing, just a huge travelling trunk that served as a table and a bed for the old man, a side table. The lighting was sparse and a bulb hanged from a precarious electrical wire from the ceiling that had peeled very badly.

At the back of the room, there were two windows covered with yellowish Yiddish newspapers dated 1942, and a low shutter had been kept opened, The evening fresh wind was coming in and the old man was shivering in his armchair, yet he made no attempt to cover himself with the heavy shawl that laid on the bed.

Through the door, was the backyard with a tiny vegetable garden, a cage with rabbits, and an old fashion water pump and old toilet room?

Every morning, the old man worked in his garden and fed the rabbits. The old man was very thin, his body emaciated, yet the stern look on his face revealed a fierce and proud soul, the light of intelligence shined in his sharp eyes.

It was 6pm; the old man was resting in his armchair, a look vacant in his eyes. Like everyday, he would take the yellowish picture, kiss it and make a silent prayer, his lips moving in cadence to the silent words of his soul.

There was no timepiece, the room was so bare and cold, yet the old man did not seem to care.

Then, unexpectedly, the door opened from the front side, the sling squealed, the front door has had not been opened for several decades now. It was without lock yet none had come into the house of the old man for decades.

Anataalie entered. She was wearing a simple and long jersey gray dress, a pearl necklace and over it a heavy shawl, like the Hungarian women of the village. Her step was firm as she entered, and with her she brought the life that has ceased to exist in this house for years.

She did not say a word; she removed her shawl and put it on the bed. She saw the old man trembling with cold, but she did not want to insult him by offering to cover him up, she knew this kind of men, they were more proud than life and death.

Anataalie had come to know about Joseph through some archives she had been researching in La Sorbonne while working on her Thesis: Post-Traumatic behaviors of acts of violence.

The tiny quote referred to Joseph after the Second World War was ended, and the concentration camps opened to the world to see how human beings had been treated. It was a horrendous discovery for those who opened the camp to the light, as it was still so for Anataalie who read the scanty details of Joseph's survival.

None really knew what had happened to Joseph, where he had re-settled, whether he was still alive, and it took Anataalie some three years before she located Joseph in this small backward village in Hungary.

She had taken the first flight, and it had been very difficult to reach the small village. None cared for its inhabitants; it was a ghostly place, made of miserable houses. Amenities were so scanty. Anataalie had taken lodging in one of the village's homes against offering of some foreign goods.

And so that evening, she walked her way down the village, the cold wind in her face, it took so much strength from her to walk against the snowy blizzard to reach the house of Joseph. None knew what he was doing, whether he was alive. None had seen him for decades or even cared to visit him.

Anataalie reached Joseph's house, the door was unlocked and there he was, as she had dreamt she would find him. An old emaciated man, with a fierce look in his eyes. As she came near to him, he had a hard look in his eyes, and cruelly planted his gaze in her eyes. She did not budge or said a word, and slowly she saw the hard stare melt into the

gaze of an old man near to death, kindly warmth filled the eyes of Joseph. He told her in French:
"You are French! "

"Yes. My mane is Anataalie, Joseph."
He asked quickly:
"What is it that you want? I have nothing left to give, to share."

Anataalie did not reply. She stood there, and went to take some water from the backside of the house and warmed it on the stove. She poured the warm water and gave it to drink to Joseph. There was nothing else to put in the water, she knew. There was but one white metal timbale and the old man drank slowly.

"Thank you." Joseph said in a very low voice.

Anataalie slowly came closer and said:
"Joseph, please do not fear me. The Star of David is but a star to me, among stars, in the sky. None can take it down. I know Joseph. Please do not fear me."

As she said the words, she came close to the side table, the old man muscles hardened, and he looked as if he were ready to hit Anataalie.

The atmosphere in the house became very tense, as it never had been before. Anataalie continued to come closer to the small table, slowly she put her hand forward, the old man's eyes became cruel.

He hated her, he said:
"No"

Anataalie replied:

"Yes, it is time Joseph. I must"

And she continued advancing her hand towards the small table, and her fingers gently took the old photograph. The old man took Anataalie's wrist and cruelly pushed his hard nails until blood ran from the white skin of Anataalie onto the photo.

Blood dripped in tiny tears over the photo and Joseph collapsed in his armchair, sobbing uncontrollably.

Anataalie took the photo and said gently:
"It is alright Joseph. Please. Be gentle for them."

Anataalie had tears in her eyes and the old man was fascinated as he looked at her taking his despair of decades between her soft white hands.

Anataalie said:
"What were their names Joseph?"

The yellow picture showed two beautiful little girls playing in the same garden with their mother.

"Danuta and Sophia." replied Joseph.

"How old where they?"

Joseph laughed hysterically and said:
"Read the back, you will know"."Girls of Paper."

Anataalie said:
"Yes, Joseph, I read."

He said:

"Then do not ask any question anymore. I have not long to live. This is what I wrote. Girls of Paper".

He continued in an extinguished voice to narrate his life as he remembered it:

"We were told by the Nazis then to wear the Star of David like a shame. And we all four said: the German are fools, we are very proud to wear it, stupid Hitler.Then my wife was a doctor, they prevented her from practicing, and then they killed her because she helped a woman in labor to deliver. They killed them all. They did not want Jewish doctors. Then they took my little girls, and they are dead too.

They came to this house and said, everything is for the German, and you have nothing. And I was taken to a concentration camp. I survived in despair, despair fed me, because I remembered that this photo I had hidden under a tile, and I lived through hell just to get back this photo.

As you see they took everything. When the war was over I came back here and never left again. I lived with the girls of paper.

Because that is what I lived for, to find my two little girls of paper."

Anataalie said softly:

"Yes, Joseph, I have come for them too. To tell the story of the little girls of paper. Of all the little girls of paper."

Now Joseph, you must come with me, in Paris. Stay at my house. And before you die, take with you some days of your life when you lived in the freedom of the world to the girls of paper.

When you will meet them in heaven, on your death, they will be at the gate, and they will ask you: Father, how is Paris? The free world? The dolls? The dresses? The flowers?

They were little girls; they did not have time to see all of these. They will ask you too how it feels to love.

You must take this with you Joseph before you die. Your life cannot be of paper; it will hurt them if you bring them a life of paper."

Joseph stood up; he was very frail, he was so old. He said:
Yes, to the little girls of paper in heaven I will bring them the breath of the free world.

The old man took the arm of Anataalie, and left the house.
-The end-

Short Story 3

The Samovar

A new lady moved in the next villa in posh Knightsbridge area of London, not very far from the luxury department stores Harrods. Harrods had been there for generations in the capital and catered to the royal family household.

But the whole place had taken a new significance since Lady Diana Spencer; Princess of Wales had become friend with Dodi, the son of the owner of Harrods. The tale of their romance did feel at the time like a typical London summer love until tragedy struck and both lost their lives in a car crash in a tunnel in Paris. Harrods was more than a department stores now; it had become somehow a landmark. Yes, the Princess had come to shop there often, and no matter on which floor you landed one always felt a fleeting sadness around the place.

Many had bought available mansions and luxury suites in the suburb, and the price of the real estate has become extravagant, even more exhorbitant than during the oil dollar boom, when wealthy Arabs bought estates at very high prices.

Somehow, the place had also caught the fancy of the richest of the Russian, and not too long ago a Russian woman had bought a large suite, located within walking distance from Harrods. The place was very British in architecture, and there was even a porter in uniform to guard the building.

And in that particular morning, the porter was already talking to his neighbor, a younger man about the new owner. He narrated:

"Yes she came, she is a very old lady, a Russian, but trust me she frightens me. She looks like a witch."

The young Irish lad laughed and exclaimed:
" Well that is a first, so far no woman you described was out of your taste. I say, she must be real ugly."

The porter felt a bit insulted and pinched his lips and stayed silent…As they continued cleaning the front porch, the porter stood up immediately, pale, and went to open the door of the lodge. Soon an old woman appeared. She had a very odd and very lonely look about her. It was spring day, but she was wearing a long black mink coat with a black toque, she had laced boots on, like the Russian army's, very polished very shiny, she had black leather gloves and a black bag.
She said:
"Thank you porter"
She gave him a crisp banknote of five sterling pounds.
The youngster thought to himself: "well not bad for just opening a door" But as he looked at the porter he found that the man did not give his shining smile as he did to others when he received a tip. Five pounds for opening the door, wow the young man approached closer, to be in the view of that woman, in case well she would find some use for him, he sure could use the money.
As he looked up at her, he too froze, she was past seventy years old, had a few hair left which obviously had been tinted jet black, she had

painted her face with a whitish cake cream foundation and her lips were bright red, a la Paloma Picasso. But what frightened him at once was the fact that she wore a black strap over her right eye, a pirate eye cover. Her smile was full with gold teeth.

He froze too: he too did not feel like looking at her.

She did not seem to care, and gingerly hailed a taxi. She looked so odd. And her voice was like a broken record, they heard her repeating no less than ten times to the taxi driver Harrods, Harrods, Harrods, as she climbed in the taxi. None of them felt like earning an extra five pounds, and they simply left her open the taxi door. She did not care, her mouth full of gold teeth was wide open and they shuddered at the sight.

Natasha was her name, and she was indeed Russian. She went to Harrods and people walked away from her…she looked like a witch and that is exactly how she had been called by: witch for a long time though. She did not seem to care, and knew the place oh too well. She went to the Boucheron jewelers and asked them to show them necklaces with fine cut diamonds, sapphire and aquamarine.

They made her sit, and offered her coffee in a fine porcelain cup. They knew her well: she was a valuable customer. After much display of jewels, she made up her mind for the loveliest and the costliest piece they had, a 55,000 Sterling pounds jewel. She instructed them to have a few extra sapphires set to the jewel. The necklace would be delivered to her suite in the evening. She said in her atoned voice:

"Thank you, do please be on time 7pm on the dot."

They smiled, she was odd, but she was an excellent customer.

Then she proceeded to the Delicatessen Floor. It was a prompt purchase, she ordered some Fois Gras and caviar and Dom Perignon. She attempted to walk a bit more in the department store, but she felt tired already.

She hailed a taxi back and came back to the Suite. The suite was posh and cozy. The two service staff, she had hired for the evening, had been sent by an agency and were working on setting the place for her soiree, they knew what she wanted.

She went to rest for a while. Downstairs, the two porters were gossiping about how repulsive her appearance was, they had never seen such a witch figure before. But then, to their utter dismay: bouquet after bouquet started to arrive for her, and the porter was kept very busy, he had counted not less than 120 bouquets so far.

" Special delivery for Madame Natasha", the delivery people would say, the porter had never seen so many flowers in his entire life.... He was puzzled. He asked the delivery people:

" From where are all those bouquets?" They always gave the same response: either a cold silence or
" We are not at liberty to say".

The porter would go to the Suite, and each time he brought a bouquet, the maid slipped a fiver in his hand. What a day for him, he never had made that much money in a year and that easily too. He started to love the witch, as he now fondly nicknamed her.

For three days they did not see her, she did not come out, but the bouquets continued coming, and the porter felt an immense love for Madame Natasha. He decided in his heart not to refer to her as a witch anymore, but called her La Grande Dame and with great reverence too.

On the third day afternoon, caterers started to bring dishes of food in porcelain and crystal balls, silver trays; a catering truck from Harrods brought it all.

That evening, Rolls Royce cars parked in front of the building and the owners were tipping the porter heavily; some people came on foot. Yes, the beautiful people as others call the rich and beautiful started arriving for La Grande Dame.

The porter showed the place to many of them and each time, he got a glimpse of La Grande Dame, she was wearing a sort of diamond tiara and lots of jewels, she sparkled a lot, and he revered her, he loved her so. She looked wonderful bejeweled. He had forgotten the witch: he loved his Grande Dame.

Soon the place was packed.

Inside Natasha welcomed each and everyone personally; all of them were white Russian: the descendants of the Tsar family. A violinist was playing tzigane melodies, and everyone was smiling back to Natasha.

Natasha was happy, but there was an intense look in the only eye that was visible, she was waiting for one more guest. It was past midnight, and at long last one more ring was heard. She jumped on her feet inspite of her age, and went quickly to open the door, pushing aside the staff.

There, at the door, stood a tall and slender young woman of twenty-five with a white skin and very long and wavy chestnut hair, she was wearing a long velvet coat of night blue with gold embroidery.

As she stood there, Natasha smiled at the young woman, and said nervously:

"Come in Anataalie; I have missed you so."

The young lady entered and embraced La grand dame, smiling and saying:
"Anoushka, I missed you too."

As Anataalie came in, everyone felt envious of her closeness to the otherwise distant Grande dame. La Grande Dame came from a very wealthy white family and her name only commanded grand respect. Anataalie was not even Russian; she was a French actress, a debutante. And they felt hurt that Natasha would prefer her to them who were for some, famed Bolshoi Stars or owned chic restaurants in London and Paris, some were bankers. Why her?

But they indeed felt the bond was strong. Yes they were intelligent and understood that the bond was indeed beyond normal comprehension, they tolerated in ignorance.
"Anataalie, come and sit besides me"
Natasha ordered.

Anataalie left her velvet cape with the maid. She wore a full-length fluid mauve jersey dress, with an open back to the waist; she was indeed a natural beauty.

Soon, the party resumed, and everyone loved the place, the food was great, the music was fabulous.

Suddenly the place grew cold and quiet, everyone felt uneasy, and everyone felt a stab in his or her heart, a sad and profound vibration. They looked towards Anataalie and Natasha, It was so strange: the tears were rolling down the powdered face of Natasha, and Anataalie was holding her hand. They were puzzled, and astonished for not once did they see Natasha cry, not once, even when everything had been taken from her then, when they left Russia like vagabonds, when her husband died, when she was told she had cancer.

Anataalie was motionless and did not attempt to console Natasha in any way, she held her hand, and said:
"Cry deeply Natasha, it must have a purpose. the tears, cry deeply…"

She held the hand of Natasha and closed her eyes for a while. She remembered. How could she ever forget? She relived that time in their past, a time that was hidden to others, and yet common only to Natasha and Anataalie: the secret bond's key.

Two years ago, she had met Vladimir in London. He had an antique shop in Kings' road and was doing well. Anataalie was shopping and she had noticed a lovely samovar that she had seen in the window display of Vladimir's place.

Immediately a friendship was struck. Both felt as if they had known each other for a long time. They talked about his life as a Russian émigré issued from an aristocracy line that did not mean a thing anymore. Her mother was a well known and a famous poetess, and a great beauty in her youth, her father had been a portraitist. Whilst they were chased from Russia by the red army, his father had secured a position as the official portraitist of the late Shah of Iran, in the house of Pavlavi. They accumulated a great wealth once again.

Her mother was a favorite in the entourage of the Empress Farah Dibah of Iran, and soon she spoke Farsi fluently. She was invited everywhere the Pavlavi family went. Natasha was of extreme beauty. Yet, Vladimir recalled with a tinge of hate in his voice, his husband, his father Fedor developed a taste for pretty ladies, and the royal family seemed to encourage this.

Natasha was very hurt, but she was a woman of great courage and never raised the subject, or confided in Vladimir who was still very young, hardly 10 years old when the conflict, the break-up in the marriage first appeared.

Soon Natasha was in great demand by the court of the Shah. Slowly rumors emerged that the Shah was a playboy and wanted Natasha as his own. He sent her present after present, which she did neither accept nor refused. She just kept them in a cupboard unopened; she did not send back replies or letters of thanks.

The Shah was annoyed that she remained so cold or irresponsive to his overtures. So he called her husband and commissioned him to make the portrait of Natasha. Fedor did not really care; he did the portrait and delivered it to the Shah against a very handsome payment.

Natasha was called once again to the royal household and was shown the portrait that the Shah had received from her Fedor. A terrible anguish struck at her heart, but she did not show it. She said:
"Your Highness, thank you for the honor, but portraits mean so very little to me."
The Shah then asked:
"What matters to you, Natasha?'

Foolishly she said:
"My heart is called Poetry and my soul Spirituality."

The Shah smiled and reveled in the personality of Natasha, she was the most beautiful and intriguing woman he had ever met on earth, and she was like a dream.

She left again with gifts, jewelry and boxes of caviar, textiles that a courtier was carrying for her, and she was driven back to the family house.

The Shah once more sent for Fedor. Fedor was happy because he was in great need of money, overnight he spent a lot on his favorite of the moment, and he had started gambling and was loosing heavily. He was hardly at home, and Natasha did not want to meet her husband while he was in this mood. They had not talked to each other in weeks.

Fedor was to come to the palace quickly he was told. Fedor shaved, put his best outfit and rushed to the Royal Household.

He was granted entry to the private chamber of the Shah almost immediately. The Shah commanded Fedor to sit, which was a great honor as everyone stood in front of His Highness. To sit in the presence of the Shah was a sign of great friendship and trust. Yes the Shah did like him, he felt glad and the hope of receiving more money filled his heart with anticipation. He had so much debt to repay, gambling debts

The Shah was composed and cold and he said:
"Fedor my friend you are a great artist. I know you are a portraitist, but you are such a great artist, surely you would know how to write me a poem if I asked you. You see my friend I have fallen deeply in love with a lady who is cold as ice."

Fedor at once replied:
"Well, Majesty, no lady ever remain cold after I wrote her a poem."

The Shah said:

"Thank you Fedor, please bring it here tomorrow. Put emphasis on the eyes of the ladies, they are like deep burning embers"

Fedor smiled. Yes he knew. Ladies'eyes, that were not so hard to put in words, he said to himself.

So he went home and put himself to task, the words came so easily to him. The next morning he went to the Shah and said there you are Majesty- the lines of the poem are written:

Your eyes fill the void
Of my heart
With burning embers
Your eyes empty the shame
Of my soul
With dew tears
Your eyes are mine
To eternity.

The Shah was pleased and paid Fedor a great amount of money. And that evening Fedor feasted with his new lover. He went gambling too, he won, he was very happy.

That evening, a courtier had come to the house of Natasha and had delivered the same poem engraved on a gold leaf. Natasha had seen her husband write those lines, She did not say a thing, and she did not let him know that she had read the lines. When the gold leaf engraved with the words came, she was overwhelmed with joy. Fedor was coming home at last. She called her son Vladimir and said:

" Vladimir we shall be happy again, a real family. I know."
She was so happy.

At the precise time she had talked to Vladimir. Fedor was in the night club, with his latest favorite, drinking and drinking when a singer came on stage and said that the Shah of Iran has written this verse for the love of his life, we have been asked to sing it around for one month every night. As the singer began to sing, Fedor immediately recognized his lines. Fedor was pleased. Ah he did not mind that the Shah said he had written the words himself. The Shah could say that, after all he had paid Fedor so generously.

The night was over, and then Fedor went home half drunk as usual. Natasha was up, looking so marvelously beautiful; Fedor felt shame in his heart. He tought: my own Natasha is the most enchanting woman, why do I not stay home, a perfect beauty. He looked at her as he looked on her the first time they met, and recalled how he fell madly in love with her. It was not so long ago, a decade.

He came close to her and he took her hand, she did not pull away. He felt glad, she had grown cold to him lately because she knew of his doings. They had not fought over it, they were just estranged. Fedor respected Natasha for her personality.

Tonight, she was ravishing, and he came closer, she said:
"Fedor, thank you, for the lovely poem".

He was puzzled:
"What are you saying Natasha? "

She pulled the gold leaf from the drawer of her desk, and read the words that were engraved on it. Then Fedor understood it all, the plot: women were sent to him to distract him away from Natasha, while all the time the Shah had set his intent on his wife. Why?

He was drank and shouted at Natasha:
"Why did you go to him? "
Nataasha was bewildered, she said:
"To whom Fedor? I do not understand you?"

Vladimir had waked up from his sleep and was crying. Fedor took the boy and threw him against the wall. Natasha was pale with intense anger, she said:
"Do never raise your hand on my son"

Fedor was mad: his beautiful wife, how they had carried on behind his back. He loved her eyes, he still did.

He took the paper cutter from the desk, grabbed Natasha by the throat and plunged it into her right eye.

That was years ago, Natasha had spent time in a private clinic in Switzerland and had taken Vladimir with her. She wore a black patch ever since over her right eye.

Fedor stayed in Iran, and continued his dissolute life. as the years went on
Vladimir had grown into a successful artist and auctioneer, He had been married too but his marriage had not worked well too, and he was divorced.

Many times, he had asked his mother:

"Mother, why do you not want to have a glass eye put on your right eye, it would look so nice."

She invariably replied:

" No. I want your father Fedor if he even came back to see for himself what had become of me."

Vladmir was sad but he respected his mother.

Then on that day, when he sold the Samovar to the French Actress, Anataalie, he knew he had fallen madly in love. She was the woman he had dreamt of. He had told Anataalie so then, like a foolish schoolboy. She would smile, and say:

"Be quiet Vladimir, we are good friends"

She had been invited often for supper and she and Natasha enjoyed each other's company a lot, they would talk for hours about Pushkin and Tolstoi. Natasha spoke French, as in all the great families of White Russia, the young ladies were taught French even before Russian.

Vladimir tried to win over the heart of Anataalie to no success. Out of frustration, Vladimir had become a womanizer and Natasha was very sad about it. She confided her fears to Anataalie, and said

"Anataalie, I have so much anguish. Vladimir is following his father's steps to nowhere."

Anataalie always replied:

"Let it be Natasha, he lives his life, live yours, everything will be all right."

But everything was not all right. Anattalie came one evening and said she had to go to Madrid for a year to do a film. Vladimir felt an immense pain in his heart, he went to his study, and took out the poem that his father, now deceased, had written. Yes it was the same one that brought so much tragedy in the life of his mother and read it aloud to Natasha

Poem

Your eyes fill the void
Of my heart
With burning embers
Your eyes empty the shame
Of my soul
With dew tears
Your eyes are mine
To eternity.

Then he stopped for a while pale and very distraught.

Suddenly he took the paper cutter, and plunged it twice, once in his right eye, the second time in his left eye.

He stood, and shouted, with blood pouring out from the pierced eyeballs:

"Natasha, Anataalie, now is the time for a great game, the game of my father: the roulette, the Russian roulette, the gambling of the heart.

He stumbled into the sitting room where Anataalie had run to Natasha, he had a small handgun in his hand and pulled the trigger. Vladimir was dead on the spot. Blood was everywhere, even on Anataalie's dress.

Anataalie and Natasha were bonded with the tie of blood; they were family of the broken heart genealogy

It had been three years since then, it felt like yesterday. Anataalie slowly opened her eyes as she felt the burning tears of Natasha dribbled over her hand. Natasha said:

"Anataalie, you are my daughter, truly. You and I, we have had the same fate, Fedor for Vladimir, and me for you. Be my daughter Anataalie"

As she spoke the words, she took out the marvelous diamond and sapphire necklace, and closed the clasp around Anataalie's neck.

"Anoushka, Anataalie said, "yes I shall be that to you. Forever."

None knew the true bond between those two women. Many were envious of the good fortune of Anataalie. Natasha was a revered woman of great wealth; everyone would be fortunate to be a friend.
"They will never know Anoushka, I promise," Anataalie whispered.

The next day, Natasha went flying to Greece to spend some time there. It was the last time they met. Natasha died while cutting a rose in her garden, the doctor said she did not suffer; it was a sudden heart attack.

Everyone was told so, but only Anataalie knew that Anoushka's heart had been in pain for longer and deeper than anyone would ever imagine. She died over a broken heart, ravaged twice by selfish and cruel men.
Anataalie took the samovar she had bought from Vladimir's shop, packed it and put it away for good in the attic. But yes, it was a good thing. La Grande Dame had died of a sudden heart attack

And for many years the Porter who worked at the Knightsbridge '
luxury building would talk of the Grand Dame, and the fortune he
made while she was there.

-The End-

SHORT STORY 4

The Drums of Africa

It was early winter, and London was freezing cold. Anataalie had been shopping in Bond Street for gifts for people she knew would celebrate Christmas. Bond Street was a great place to find the highest quality as well as prestige brands. She had seen earlier at her favorite jewelers' window display, some beetles brooches, Egyptian in 18 carats gold and sapphires, they were lovely and unique. Her friends would love those. She had arrived at the jewelers, they had just opened.

As she entered, the manager of the shop welcomed her with great warmth. After all she was a regular customer. He called immediately for a tea tray. Anataalie was used to the courtesy of this gentleman, and so she relaxed into the sofa chair, and removed her white kid gloves to pick up the fine porcelain cup of tea.

The manager could not help noticing on her fingers the rings he had sold her over the last three years. On her manicure hands, the diamond rings set with several solitaire diamonds, turquoises and emeralds were as dazzling and beautiful as ever. Boucheron was indeed the best jeweler there was in the world. Today the young French woman had worn only fresh water pearls on her ears and neck. She looked ravishing. It warmed the heart of the manager to see that lovely women were wearing items from his shop. Anataalie was certainly a walking advertisement; she looked stunning in those.

Anataalie drank her lemon tea slowly while the manager showed her the Egyptian artifacts she wanted.

"Yes, that will do, how many do you have presently in stock? "Natalie asked.

The manager gleefully said:
"Just four, mademoiselle"

Anataalie said softly:
"So I shall take the four. Just add the wrapping separately, I will do the wrapping myself."

The manager smiled: he knew that she wanted it this way...and he was only too willing to oblige such a courteous customer.

As the shop assistant was instructed to pack as Anataalie as requested, the Manager took advantage of the free moment to show Anataalie a new piece, a recent arrival: a forearm snake type bracelet...It had an intrinsic handwork, and Anataalie looked at it for a while, and asked:
"How much? "

The manager told the price. Anataalie said:
"Yes I want it too, but this one please have it wrapped up."

The manager laughed and said:
"Yes, we always do wrap the gifts you make to yourself, and we spare no efforts in doing so"

Anataalie gave back a brief smile. It was enough, the Manager knew that Anataalie was a discreet and mysterious woman: she never gave anything of herself readily, even a smile. But he liked her a lot, she always knew what she wanted, and she was easy to deal with, and very kind. She always inquired about his wife and children.

As they were in the process of completing the purchase, suddenly the face of the manager froze. The security men were going hurriedly towards the entrance door. Anataalie casually glanced towards the cause of the commotion.

There, in the doorway a. tall black skinned man, of over 6-ft stood motionless. He made a strange impression because of his height but also for the fact that he was dressed with a sort of cape where there was only one opening for the head and for the arms. It was of brown rough fabric, very much like a blanket and the man wore only a pair of open sandals. Anataalie immediately felt the cold invading her as she shivered for the man. How did he walk around in those open sandals, the London winter is very freezing, he would surely catch his death. His cloth came only to the calves of his legs and his arms were bare. He had around his strong neck a cord with an animal tooth, so it seems. She could not see much more as the man was chased away.

Soon after, an English lady entered the shop; she was wearing an interesting hat that was pleasing to Anataalie. She seemed nice enough, but from the strained face of the manager, Anataalie could understand that she was not an easy customer to please.

Anataalie was done, she bade farewell to the Manager but the Manager insisted to accompany Anataalie to the door, much to the annoyance of the lady. The Manager said:
" I wish an excellent day and I shall convey your wishes to my wife."

As she went into the Bond Street, she realized how cold it was, she was wearing a jersey suit of mauve color with a white kid jacket and gloves and boots, yet she felt so very cold…She had never felt that cold on previous winters.

It was just eleven o'clock in the morning and many people were walking in Bond Street. She was shivering and she thought that she had time to go to the Italian restaurant to take some warm drink. She entered, and the waiter greeted her. He was a charming young man, having an eye for pretty ladies. He always courted Anataalie when she was there, messing around her, like he did to no other customer. Anataalie smiled, he was happy.

She said:
" Alberto, please I am feeling cold, I need a very hot cappuccino"

It was a busy place, but she could hear Alberto making an Italian joke about Anataalie being cold, how he could resolve the problem…she did not mind, she was used to him, he meant no insult. He was a good man, a bit of a playboy like all Italians. Soon he brought her coffee and she took her cup in her two hands so that the warmth would reach her heart faster.

As she was drinking, she noticed that Alberto was pacing nervously the aisle up and down, with an angry face. She was puzzled, because Alberto was always in a pleasant mood. She had never seen him that upset.

She called him and told Alberto:
"I am going to refresh myself, please I need one more coffee and a croissant."

She had already stood up and he was pleased to find her so close to him. She was tall and slender, her skin was so perfect, her smile, her hair, and he was so taken by her. He could smell her perfume; she always wore that perfume…. What a beautiful woman, Alberto thought, how come she always is alone. Not once did he see her accompanied by a man…Many had tried while she had been here on previous occasions to court her, but she always remained so aloof. Even Sergio, the owner of the restaurant, was crazy about her, but she laughed him away, gently. Alberto pondered often about this: Sergio was really attracted by Anataalie and Sergio had a lot of money too, everyday he was making a fortune from this restaurant, still she did care for his advances or declarations of love. She would even refused when Sergio gave orders that her bills be on the house, she insisted to pay, always.

Anataalie walked past other tables on her way to the Powder Room. As she did she was surprised to see that the same tall black man that had been ousted from the jeweler's shop a little while ago, was seated at one of the table by the wall, on his own.

His back was to her so she moved on and climbed down the stairs to go to the bathroom. She refreshed herself, and yes now she understood why Alberto was angry. Italians are a bit racist and did not take well to darker skins. As she came up she found that the black man was still seated, his eyes flashing with anger staring at Alberto.

She understood the conflict right away. It was easy to understand why Alberto was annoyed: well, the black man was eating with his hands: he had ordered a rear T-bone steak and blood was dripping from the corner of his mouth too. Not a pretty sight. And other customers were moving away from this aisle of the restaurant to other tables.

Somehow. Anataalie felt sorry. The black man looked so alone, so isolated. He was a man like every other.

As she arrived by the black man's table, she asked:
"Do you mind if I seat here and have my coffee? "

To Anataalie' s great surprise the black man spoke in perfect English and replied:
"By all means, Miss, make yourself comfortable."

She signaled Alberto to bring her coffee and croissant over to the black man's table. Alberto was furious. As he did so, Anataalie looked him in the eyes and flashed him a smile, Alberto was happy and went away singing.

The black man was no fool, he said:
"It seems you have overpowered the angry idiot very easily."

Anataalie controlled herself, because as the black man spoke, she could see real close his smile: his teeth bloody from the T-bone steak still in his hand. It was no pretty sight, but Anataalie's face remained placid. She deliberately smiled and drank her coffee nonchalantly. The black man said:
"You are not from England, your accent is different, where are you from? "

Anataalie replied:
"I was born in France. My name is Anataalie."

The black man smiled and said:
"I am glad to have met you Anataalie, my name is Mobutu."

Anataalie replied:
"This name sounds very familiar, somehow."

Mobutu said:
"In Europe, I do not know, but in Africa yes, our family name is well known. My father is a king in African land; I am his eldest son. I am studying law here. I am in my second year."

She listened to the warm tone of his voice and casually asked:
"Yes, how do you like the place?"

Something in her wanted him to talk; the sound of his voice soothed her in a way that was hard to describe. Mobutu said:
" I have no opinion, my father told me to come here and study, and that is exactly what I am doing. Besides this, I know nothing. I form no opinion, what for?"

Anataalie recognized in this man, a strong will and pride. Mobutu had finished his meal and Alberto came to remove the dishes and clean the bloody mess on the table, murmuring Italian insults in his breath. Mobutu looked at him furiously.

Anataalie had finished her coffee and Alberto asked:
"Do you want another one, it is so cold?

Before she could answer, Monbutu asked:
"How much is a coffee?"

Alberto told him dryly the cost to which Mobutu ordered:
"Then, bring one for Mademoiselle Anataalie."

Alberto sneered:

"And for you?"

"No, I said bring one for the lady."

Alberto's face was red and Anataalie knew he was ready to explode. So she said: "Alberto, it is nice, yes I would love to accept a coffee from Mr.Mobutu at the sole condition that Mr.Mobutu accepts a tea from me."

The black man smiled and said:
"Yes, of course. Thank you. Anataalie."

Anataalie felt sad that he apparently did not have big means to live here, and she felt so cold, remembering how he went in winter, with open sandals. She wished she could do something for him, but she already knew it would be an insult to Mobutu. She kept quiet.

The coffee and tea came promptly. As they drank, Mobutu said:
"Anataalie, did you sit here because you felt sorry for me? "

Anataalie looked deeply in the eyes of the man: she said,
"Well in a way yes, because you see to be in a place and not to con-form to its ways of living can be hard."
Mobutu asked:
"What do you mean?"

Anataalie said:
"Well, you do not dress like British people."

Mobutu replied curtly:
"And when they come to my country, they do not dress like us, rather they want to force us to wear their trousers and jeans."

Anataalie retorted with a twinkle in her eyes:

"Ah Mobutu, you eat with your hands. You are an intelligent man, do not fool me with your ready made explanation. That much you understand, yes?"

Mobutu smiled and replied proudly:

"Well, Anataalie, my hands are clean, probably cleaner than their so called clean forks and knives."

Anataalie said:

"Yes, so you do not want to play by their rules, and you get stressed unnecessarily."

Mobutu said:

"Yes. Everyday I may be stressed, but stress is no big deal for me. What matters to me is that I do never betray our own traditions for my own comfort. I am the son of a king. They may treat me like a pauper here…but the blood in my veins is the blood of a king. I shall never bow my head."

Mobutu looked into Anataalie's eyes. He paused pensively for a while:

"Anataalie, I saw you earlier, I felt like talking to you, but they would not let me in that shop. Did you see me?"

Anataalie replied:

"Yes, Mobutu, I did see you there Why did you want to see me? It is strange."

He said:

" It may be strange to you yet. Yes, I had to talk to you; you are so different from others. As you walked, I could see only you, none else. Something in you called on me."

Anataalie smiled and said:
"Maybe it is because I wore a purple suit with white. Maybe I was the attractive woman you always dreamt of meeting."

Mobutu looked serious and did not take to the joke, he said:
"Anataalie, I am the son of a king, the guardian of our ancient traditions and wisdom, I know much about the ills of the soul…You are in great pain."

Anataalie lowered her eyes, felt a sharp stab in her heart. She thought for a while, and said: "Mobutu, pain is part of life."

Mobutu said:
"Why do you evade me? You know what I mean: your soul is wounded, your heart has been bled dry…. I could feel your aura from where I was. You are all kindness, yet also all pain, tell me about it Anataalie. Please."

The please from the lips of the son of a foreign king felt like another stab in her heart. Anataalie said:
"Mobutu, I cannot talk those things here."

He said:
"Yes, you can. Drink your coffee slowly, and when you feel the warm liquid finding its way in you, feel how it dissolves all your frights, open up to me. I want to help you, really. "
His face was tense, his eyes lit with a deep light as if coming from the depth of times.

Anataalie drank her coffee slowly; she felt well, safe with Mobutu…His face was gentle inspite of the traditional carvings they made on his cheeks. He had very intelligent and compassionate eyes.

She said:
"Mobutu, you have come too late. The pain cannot be taken away, my soul has absorbed it like a sponge. It is too late now."

He said:
"I know, you are in terrible pain, for how long more Natalie?"

As he said this he started beating the top of the table gently, and a gentle soothing drumbeat like was heard only by them both. She understood.

She stood up, looking at him very hard in the eyes, his look was very pained and tears were falling down his cheeks. She said:
"Yes, Mobutu. Yes."

That night, she went home. Her flat was very beautiful; she used to describe it jokingly to some of her invitees that congratulated her on her sense of interior design, as a sanctuary for wounded blue birds.

She went to take a long scented bath, and put her most dazzling light blue dress, she made her hair up and added Austrian crystal pin….

It was midnight. She went to lie on her bed. She closed her eyes, gently.
As she did she went into a deep sleep…There, in the depth of her sleep; she reached the dream where Mobutu had been waiting for her. He was there in Africa, he had drums made of camel skin, soft skin, and he started the drum beat, a call sent to her, a call returned by her heartbeat…. He was

at the drums for long, sweating heavily, his arms tensed by the effort...he played the drums harshly urging her soul purge herself from the pain...it proved impossible.

Anataalie was covered in sweat and was convulsing under the pain that was being disturbed in her soul...she screamed with anguish...

Mobutu came towards her, she saw the sad and pained look in his eyes, the drumbeat went slow, and she realized that she and he had arrived to a new place, a water pond. As she looked into the water, she saw a reflection of a new birth: she was a deer with a broken leg, a royal Bengal tiger was ready near by to pounce and eat her alive.

Then she saw Mobutu reaching for his arch; he took one arrow, and aimed at the heart of the tiger. The arrow killed the tiger on the spot and he died almost instantly in a last huge roar...As the tiger died, Anataalie at last felt her soul at ease, all the pain was gone...she felt so light, so happy.

Then she turned her trusting deer eyes towards Mobutu, he was crying as he aimed at her heart; she died without a noise.

In London, at the same time, Anataalie heard, after the echoes of the drum beat, a dull silence. Then she felt an unendurable pain in her heart, her body tensed, she remembered Mobutu kind eyes, and said:
"Thank you Mobutu, May God bless you always."

Her heart has stopped beating. She was no more.

In some furnished flat in London, one English man knocked angrily on his neighbor's door. A tall dark-skinned man opened the door, he was in tears.

The English man said:

"Mr.Mobutu, please do not beat your drums at night, my kids cannot sleep…You do not seem alright too… Is they're anything the matter?"

The blackman replied:" No John, everything is fine, I won't play drums for a long while". Good night.

SHORT STORY 5

Never drink the blood of an Arabian Falcon

A four-wheel jeep was driving hard among the sand dunes of the Arabian Desert. It was so very hot.

Anataalie, a young French businesswoman, had wanted to visit some friends in their chalet by the sea.

It had been a long time since she drove that far alone, since the Gulf War.

Whenever she visited the tiny Emirate of Kuwait, she would avert looking at the sea-line beyond the road. The nightmarish memories were still too present: many women had walked into the sea never to return...They walked to a destiny in the sea, seeking purification from the acts of hatred committed from both sides.

Anataalie remembered one fragile shadow clothed in the black abbaya of respect, getting deeper into the water, getting lost in the line where the sky and the sea meet, drowning itself to oblivion

Anataalie had come on business trip, and she had been invited by her friends to stay with them at their chalet. This coastline has been cleared and cleansed from the mines and the oil pollution and all stigmas of an absurd war, they said. Yet, nothing had truly changed, the air was heavy with anguish and hatred.

Her friend Ayman was a university teacher and her husband was a psychiatrist, they had just finished their education in the United States, and were very busy in trying to help construct a better society in their homeland.

They had come home to find an opulent country where previously hardly any crime was ever committed, now under assault from minds disturbed by the traumas of war. Everyday, there were new incidents. Both had become very active in their jobs, it was a national duty, they said.

Every Thursday and Friday, the couple would leave the main city and stay at their chalet by the sea, where everything was calm, quiet and safe.

Anataalie had arrived to Kuwait on business, and she wasted no time working on closing the business deal she had come for. Now she was free to avail the couple's invitation and she set herself in her jeep and started her journey.

The weather was cooler and there was movement on the road, opulence has returned, but it was not the same. People did not smile so easily. Here and there, she would find people staring at her with blank hatred, She knew the look, it was the war looks all over again. She did not mind them anymore.

She drove, the car phone rang: It was Ayman:

"Hi Anataalie, are you ok? Is everything fine? "

"Yes, I am fine, I will reach your place within 10 minutes" Anataalie assured her friend.

"Great, replied Ayman, "I have your favorite desert prepared: konafe". Konafe was indeed an Arabian dish, but Palestinian, it was done with camel milk nuts and cheese.

Anataalie took a brief look on her vehicle's back seat: yes, the huge basket of Saudi Arabian dates she had bought at Al Samadi ,a luxury shop in Salmiayah. Gifting was part of the customs of this region.

As her attention focused once again on the trail, she saw a caravan of camels walking slowly. She loved watching as she stopped her jeep. Camels do not run, they walk slowly, carelessly, the bigger first, and then one by one so it seems to the smallest. The newly born camels were last and it was a large group.

She watched, smiling to herself, the tiny camels were adorable, and she laughed. She remembered how once a camel had spit in her face because it liked her.

As she was lost in her thought, she found that somehow, the camels started to walk faster, it was unusual, in fact their pace quickened considerably all of a sudden. Then she saw an old man and his companions mounted on camels with scanty goods attached to the sides of the camels. They were angry, and came towards Anataalie's jeep and asked:
"What are you doing here?"
Anataalie replied:
"What is it to you?"

They said:
"You are a foreigner, what are you doing in our way?

Anataalie looked straight at the chief and said:

"Where are your manners? Why are you in my way? The desert does not belong to you."

The old man remained silent and said:
"Forgive me, I was rude. Please go with my wives take some coffee and dates with us."

Anataalie knew it would be rude and perhaps careless to refuse. She replied:
"Thank you, I am honored."

The old man gave a sign to the rest of the caravan, and the women dismounted the camels and set up the tent along with their young sons, all were below 12 years old. Soon the coffee was boiling, and Anataalie sat with the women in one side while the old man was sitting with the young boys on the other side of the tent.

The women asked:
"Where are you from?"

Anataalie replied:
"From France."

They continued:
"Yes, we heard that it is a nice country"

Anataalie drank her coffee in silence. She was puzzled; the women were old and tired and wore ragged clothes. There was no food offered. Again they enquired:
"Why are you here?"

Anataalie said:
"I came for business."

The women shook their heads:
" Yes, we can see you are smart."

And they refilled her cup with coffee. Anataalie asked:
"Where are the other men?"

The women kept silent, then the oldest said:
"Sister, you know this land. You know what happened. Why do you ask those questions? Do you not guess?"

Anataalie replied.
"I dare not guess any longer. I dare not dream any longer, I dare not speak any longer. Tell me."

The older women said:
"You know that we Bedouins had remained attached only to our bloodline, not to any land or any rule as such though we respected everyone. During the war, we were hunted us down, many of my sons died. We all had been born in this land on this side of the border, and yet none would recognize us. And we were chased from every side. We had no money, no food, no school, and no medical care. None wanted us. They say we are Be-douin (without land), as if we do not exist.

We suffered greatly. During the war, everyone took us as his or her enemies, there were no friends and no place left for so and us we went deeper in the desert, to be safe. There was no water, no food, nothing. And so I had only one son, a grown up son.

His father, this old man was sick, my other children were infants. We were famished. We did not steal.

So my elder son was sent with a camel and our last can of water outside to search for food, for rodents, for snakes, anything to eat. to save us
from a sure death. The war was over, we were told, and the father said:

"Yes, let him go. It is his duty now as our only grown up son left, to go
and find food. I am too tired and you women sleep with the children. It
is safer now".

Hamad, our only adult son left us and promised to come soon with
food.

He looked and looked everywhere; there was no food. Other
Bedouins were in the same situation. None would help him either.

Hamad wandered on the desert until at last he found a tent from a
rich man, Yusuf. There, Hamad saw abundance of food and water.
Hamad approached the rich man and asked him: "Brother, give me
food, we are starving."

Yusuf had him beaten up just for asking and coming near. Hamad
left that place all bruised, his heart filled with anguish and mistrust. He
only asked for Arab hospitality, why did he get beaten up? He was so
confused.

He cried, a man's tear in the desert and then he remembered that he
could not go home without food, he was to try harder. He waited by
Yusuf's tent to see that when he left perhaps in the garbage left behind
he could find a meal for us.

He just waited to find our meal in the garbage of the rich man.

The rich man has had long last left, but nothing at all he had left
behind. As he stepped in his wheel-drive with his drivers and servants,
Yousuf's gaze searched the horizon for Hamad, and spat at his sight.

Hamad felt as if that night would never end. His heart sank, there was nothing at all, not even the seed of a date chewed by Yusuf, he had taken everything away, on purpose. He had made his servant clean up the desert so that Hamad could find nothing at all.

Hamad mounted his camel and started on his way back. Astonished, he found himself once again on the trail of, Yousuf's convoy.

Yusuf had opened the window of the jeep and was letting his falcon fly free to find him a prey, a trophy to show his friends back on the city.
Hamad saw the bird. It was a beautiful falcon and very smart too. Hamad loved falcons. This one was so healthy; it brought joy to his heart.

Hamad decided to follow the falcon; falcons could always spot a meal. It would not be stealing; Hamad would just be quicker and take the first prey before the falcon descended on it. The falcon could always find another one.

The falcon was circling and circling. The falcon's eyes scrutinized the desert for a prey, and so far there was none. Then the falcon gave a huge shriek in the silence of the desert and descended madly towards Hamad.

Hamad understood that the falcon had come to attack him and so he quickly wrapped his hand with his head cloth, and watch the ferocious falcon descend on him.

Its beak was sharp, he tore up the skin of Hamad's face, blood was dripping…Hamad knew the weakness in the falcon, he quickly wiped the blood from his face with his hands wrapped in cloth, soon the cloth was soaked in blood and Hamad kept his hand offered, the falcon came down circling again with a killing shriek and came to prey on Hamad's hand.

All happened very fast. Hamad's hand had caught the falcon neck and strangled it to death.

Hamad fell on the ground exhausted, he had to replenish the loss of fluid from the body, and he had no water. He took his knife and made an incision in the throat of the inert falcon and drank the falcon blood.

He felt so much better; he slept for ten minutes, having secured the prey, the dead falcon under him. Then he got up and rushed back to the family tent, he narrated his ordeal.

None spoke, the falcon was quickly roasted and the family had something to eat for today.

Everyone fell asleep sound, their stomach quieted with the flesh of the falcon, It had been a delicious meal, the bird was well nourished and the meal was abundant.

In the morning, army men entered their poor tent. Yusuf was with them: he pointed out to Hamad.

Without a word, they dragged Hamad in the open, and before the old man could rise from his couch, a bullet was heard.

As they came out, the body of Hamad was left on the desert ground, and the police starting to depart.

The old man asked:
"Why?"

The army man replied:

Why do you ask old man? Your son had done something very wrong. He drank the blood of the Arabian falcon that did not belong to him, this crime is punishable and it is death penalty

The old man fell on his knees and cried:

"What justice, you leave us like animals, no food, no school, and no medicine. Was my son of less value than a vulgar bird?"

The army man said:

"Old man, please keep quiet. The war has taken all the pity away from the people's heart. None will hear you, pray, that is all. I cannot help you."

They left. Ever since, the old man would go every night out to look for birds and shoot them down."

Anataalie said to the women.

"Yes, life is hard, for the men, and the falcons, and the desert and the land of Arabia."

Anataalie said:

"Tonight. Please. Tell the old man not to go out. Please take the sweets in my car. Can you come tomorrow to the city to take provisions from me? "

The women said:

"No. We are Bedouins; they would shoot at us."

Then Anataalie rose and said:

"Tomorrow at this time, be here, I will bring you provisions for two seasons. Every two seasons you will meet here, or there will be someone who will show you this pendant. You will receive food from me. This is our secret. Now tell the old man, and ask him to stop shooting the birds."

The woman went to the old man, and they talked. The old woman said.

" Yes, he thanks you. Everytime he shot a bird he felt bad in his heart. He said: "God be with you."

Then, let it be our secret: God be with you."

Anaatalie replied as she left and drove away to her friends' house.

Soon she had reached the Chalet. It was a place full of luxury, there was also a boat berthed nearby.

Ayman and her husband Misha'al were very pleased to have her and they talked and talked. Suddenly Misha'al rose and smiled broadly:

"Did you see my latest craze?"

As Anataalie looked up she saw Mishaal wearing leather shield on his right arm, and he had brought out a beautiful falcon. Misha'al said:

"One of my patients had given it to me. He is a rich man, and he never recovered when a savage Bedouin had killed one of his birds, can you believe those primitive people killing a defenseless bird.

Anataalie asked:

"Where is your patient, who is he?"

Misha'al replied:

"Does it matter? He has left months ago for treatment in London. He won't be back anytime soon."

-theEnd.

SHORT STORY 6

The Death of the French Archeologist

It was night in Upper Egypt, it was very very hot, the crickets were flying around the empty tent of the lone French Archeologist, Monsieur Lucien. His electric lamp had attracted millions of fireflies; snakes were crawling around looking for the foolish rodents that would attempt to go for the crumbs of bread left in the tent from Lucien's last meal.

The tent was lonely, there were no sign of human life and the place did feel equally desolate except for that open electric eye in the night: the battery lamp hanging on the top of the tent

Lucien had come here two weeks ago. He had planned his expedition carefully and he believed firmly that he would find the tomb of a pharaohness forgotten in the pages of history, and human memory. He had worked back in La Sorbonne Libraries for years, and had finally made his mind to carry on that expedition.

It was easy for him, the French Government of Culture was sponsoring his efforts and he had obtained a handsome grant. Lucien was well known in the archeology circle for his fine studies on Egyptian history: he was a brilliant historian and a most remarkable archeologist. He had been on numerous expeditions in Iraq, and Al Sharaqat, he had masterminded many expeditions in Egypt, but did never get to Egypt, this would be his first trip to Egypt. It was peculiar that such a brilliant Egyptologist had never set foot in the land of the Pharaohs and instead spent time on other lands in Mesopotamia…

He was forty-five, his health was not so robust, he had worked too hard, his trips abroad took their toll on his health, and his recent divorce had left him rather weakened.

But he had finally made it to that spot in the land of the Pharaohs, and that is all that he had been concerned. He had hired a few locals and they drove with jeeps through the desert lands.

Everything went well, Lucien wore the Egyptian dishdasha, ate Egyptian food, fool medanes, kuboouzz, and learnt to bear the heat by covering his head with a cloth like turban. He felt tired but happy that everything went so well. Until that spot where there was some marking on the land.

The locals did not want to go any further, and Lucien told them that it was there precisely where they would have to dig and get paid for their efforts. None wanted to know anything, they did not care for the money or their life for that matter: they simply run away on foot through the desert land They became crazed with grief and the echo of their wailing traveled long and far as Lucien drove on in the jeep, all alone now.

He reached the precise spot he had earmarked on his archeological map and proceeded to put his tent up. It was night, and he wanted to rest and wake early in the morning to dig by himself. He did not know how he would do so, but he knew he would have to do it.

But the night was full of nightmares for him, he heard a female voice calling his name in sobs, and he started trembling and sweating. He got up, drank some water, filled his backpack with tools and food and decided to go in the night to meet the call of his nightmare. He knew that this was totally absurd but he felt compelled to go and he went.

He drove to that exact spot: it looked like a sand dune, but as he started removing with his spade some of the sand, he found that all the sands of time eerily came down to reveal a beautiful engraved turquoise grave with the portrait of a young Egyptian girl. The adornments were in gold, and he was shocked to see how easy he had found the tomb of a forgotten Pharaohnesss.

He pushed the door, it was not even locked, and it just opened. And he proceeded to descend into the vault. He switched off his car light, so the battery would not be down, he did not know yet how long the first leg of his discovery would take, so he took his light only and descended….

As he did so, he heard a heavy noise the door had closed on him, and he suddenly realized that he had been trapped alive in the tomb of the young pharaoness.

Somehow and eerily so, he felt it was the fate closing the last door on him, he was home again. The tomb was magnificent and he knew that there was no use of cataloguing anything even mentally because this was too the last leg of his travel in this mortal life.

He sat besides the sarcophagi of the pharaoness, and closed his eyes to prepare for his final sleep.

As he fell asleep, memories of his childhood came back to him, flooding his heart with a long ago memory of a pain that did never heal: it all came back to him now…

He had been born in a typical French bourgeois house, his mother was a beautiful actress, so gracious, so talented. His father was a heart surgeon. Soon his father became abusive and showed signs of mental imbalance and he deserted the family mansion to go with other women. Soon, he did not even bother to show up any more in their house. He remembered how little it mattered to anyone that his father was no more coming to visit him or her, or cared for them. Everyone was told that the brilliant brain surgeon had gone abroad to work for a king as a private doctor, and that he would visit occasionally.

One day his mother called him and said:

"Lucien come here, I have to go away for a while on an acting tour, you are thirteen, and you know your father is no good for you, so we shall tell none about this. I am going away on an acting tour and you will make sure that the house is kept in good order, that your brother and sister go to school, all the bills will be paid by the bank, there is lots of money in the safe, this is the combination. If someone asks for me just tell him or her that I am sick with the flue, that is all."

Lucien asked:

"Mother do you have to go?"

She looked deeply in his eyes and said gravely with a gentle smile:

"Yes Lucien I must go. Today. Now go to school. Oh I forgot this is very important, I have kept some caviar from Russia in the deep freezer, please do never open it, because it will get spoilt, just a little bit of air or light will spoil this caviar, and I want to have it when I come back. So take care, do never open the deep freezer."

He went to school and as he came home she was gone, there was no trace of her, yet all her things were around, weeks went by, months, until one day he had need for money and he opened the safe, there was an envelope that read: To Lucien, take this to the mayor on your 18th birthday.

He did not understand, but she was his mother and he had no right to question her motives or desires. He received post cards from her from different places, on which she wrote that she needed a bit more time and to do as she said.

On the day of his eighteenth birthday, Lucien woke up and the first thing he did was to go to the safe and take the envelope to the Mayor.

The Mayor was a friend of his mother, some said he had loved her once. He was an old man now, and he took the envelope and read the contents of a blue Yves Saint- perfume scented letter, and tears fell from his eyes.

He said:"
Lucien, you will have to be brave, your mother is no more."
Lucien said:
" No, Monsieur, you must be mistaken, I have received postcards from her all the time, even yesterday"
The Mayor had already left his seat and had requested the Mortician and two policemen and an attorney to come at once to his office and they proceeded to the house of Lucien.
Lucien thought they were all mad, but as he opened the door, the mayor asked Lucien, "Please tell your sister and brother to stay in their room and come and show me where the deep freezer is"

Lucien's heart beat faster and he run in the pantry room and showed the deep freezer, the mayor was sobbing as he opened the deep freezer, there she was in her beautiful blue dress, she was as beautiful as ever, the deep freezer had kept her as she had always been, a beauty queen.

Lucien fainted

He remained ill for some times, then he was sent to Paris to study at La Sorbonne. He wanted to study Mummies; the mummification process and he had become the most brilliant archeologist of Paris.

Now he knew that life has come full circle, and that in a way he was rejoining his mother 's soul by being locked in this secret tomb, at last peace came over his soul as he fell asleep near to his beautiful mother, never to wake up again: Anataalie, the Pharaoness, his mother in turquoise...

-The End-

SHORT STORY 7

The Viennese Ball

It was autumn in Vienna.

Anataalie had flown all the way from the Middle East where she run her own company, to spend just one night in Vienna and attend the opening of the Viennese Balls' season

She had met a few years ago, the Commercial Attaché of the Austrian Embassy in Dubai: a gentleman, Dr. Wolfgang Danz and his wife, Lisa, who was known to be a great musician. She played the violin in such a delightful way.

They were well known in the Middle East for their hospitality and the great dinner parties they organized. Of course, musicians were always there. Business was growing between Austria and the Middle East and Swarowski Austrian Crystals had become a house name for any oriental lady. Dr Danz and his wife had brought over, several times over the years they spent in the Middle East, the entire Viennese Ball to Dubai. It was always a resounding success.

It was an amazing event in Vienna was awaited with great anticipation by many. Anataalie had been invited in one of those Arabian Viennese Balls, she remembered it well.

That very first time in Dubai, Anataalie had dressed with particular care; she had a ball gown flown in especially from a Paris Couture House for that event. She asked her driver to take her to the Hilton Hotel ballroom.

As she entered the ballroom, Something struck her sharp in the heart: The Valses de Strauss played live by an Austrian orchestra, and dancing couples were swirling across the dance floor. It was as if she had entered another time dimension.

She had not really planned to attend this event, as she had been so very busy. The wife of Dr.Danz, Lisa, had called on her personally and had insisted so much that she should be present for that special evening. Lisa was a handsome woman of forties, always well dressed, she said:

"Well, Anataalie, what is the matter? Just drop by, put a simple dinner dress, have something to eat with us, a toast whatever, just come. I promise I won't push you in the arms of a lone dancer."

Anataalie had laughed, she liked Lisa a lot, and she was indeed such a charming lady and such a delightful artist too:

"Fine, Lisa, I will drop by for half an hour if you promise me that you will not try to keep more than this. I do have a lot of work to complete. You know that if it were at all possible, I would certainly like to attend the full ball, and even fly every season to Vienna like I used to do."

Lisa replied firmly:
"Alright, Anataalie, you have my word."

So it was agreed. Anataalie was unusually very busy at this time of the year: she had more work than she could handle. Her business has grown very quickly, and she had to work practically day and night to meet all the deadlines that kept piling in front of her. But work did not frighten her, she liked working.

So that evening, she went to the Ballroom of the Hilton Hotel, and as she entered, a Filipino waitress came immediately to free her from her long night blue velvet cape. She was wearing a stunning yet plain lilac lace ball gown and her diamond necklace and bracelets enhanced the natural elegance of her outfit.

Soon behind the Filipino waitress, she saw Lisa and Dr Danz coming her way, they were glowing with happiness, and Anataalie became aware of the exquisite music that was being played in the ballroom.

As they took her in, she was introduced to a few people, but the sight mesmerized Anataalie: they were a dozen of couples dressed in fabulous attires waltzing away the Arabian night. It was entrancing, and she kept looking at the couples.

Dr.Danz laughed, teasing her a bit:
"I bet you do not care about work now"

Anataalie gave a gentle smile:
"Yes, you are right. But we have an agreement here, yes? Half an hour, that is all I can manage, you know that. Besides I am not dressed to dance."

Dr Danz pulled her by the hand unto the dance floor and said:
"Oh yes, you are Anataalie."

Anataalie was taken for a dance and it pleased her that she was the only one in a colourful dress where everyone else was wearing pure white. She laughed:

"I knew, you would kidnap me or something."

But Dr.Danz was a professional man, and he knew that Anataalie had much work, and that it would be a mistake to keep her here, behind schedule, and so he brought her back to his wife Lisa.

Lisa was glowing with pride:

"Anataalie, you are a sensation. Everyone has asked me about you.

Anataalie smiled:

".... And you did not say a thing, right? We have an agreement, Lisa, remember?"

Lisa replied with a twinkle in her eyes:

"Yes, of course Anataalie. Not a word. You are the invisible one, the Cinderella of Arabia, you will disappear at twelve midnight as in the fairy tale"

Anataalie said:

"Lisa I must go, it was very nice, it felt like a breath of fresh air. You have done a splendid job. Now, I must really go."

Lisa and her husband said:

" Of course, thank you for having found the time to come and see us. You know how much we love your company."

She left and went back to the city. She had so much work and she decided to go to her office and work for a while longer. The building was silent and the watchman wished her a good evening. He was used to Anataalie working long hours. It was not unusual for her to work late nights.

When her work was over, she went home. The day was done, like yesterday, and everyday before.

A few months had passed. Dr.Danz had been transferred to another country as Ambassador of Austria, somewhere in Africa and she had bade them farewell. Lisa had grown used to Anataalie and treated her like a daughter. She cried when she took her final leave from her. Anataalie promised that whenever they were in Salzburg, she would visit them.

It was more than a year since she last saw them. Then she received a call in her office. She had been as usual very busy running her company and felt very stressed by the work. When she heard the voice of Lisa, she felt happy and remembered that half an hour of the Viennese Ball of Dubai that had meant more to her than she could understand herself.

Lisa said:
"Well Anataalie, we are in Salzburg for a vacation. It is so good to be home. I have lovely grand children, you know. And so, well, I am calling you because there is a Viennese ball and I am the one to take care of it all. It is a big event, and we expect royalties to attend, even Princess Diana, Princess Stephanie.

Anataalie laughed:
"Yes, Lisa, why does this not surprise me? I am so terribly busy…"

Lisa interrupted her:

"Anataalie, not again. Come to Austria. Life is short. Come and dance a few nights away. Your company will not collapse for this. If you were sick what would happen?"

Anataalie laughed:
"All right Lisa, I will fly to Salzburg for a night."

Lisa said:
"Please stay at our house, I see so little of you"

Anataalie replied:
"No Lisa, it is best if I stayed in a hotel. I will be getting business calls and faxes and I really do not want to bother you with that. No I will stay in a hotel. Yes, I will be there."

The phone call ended. Everything was fixed; Anataalie would be flying to Austria for a night, for a valse.

And there she was: it had been a long flight, but when she landed in Salzburg, the crisp cold wind revived her and she knew that she loved the city already.

She had brought with her a most magnificent gown, this time of pure traditional snow-white organza, embroidered and studded with Austrian crystal beads. And she had on a long white velvet cape in the same design. She looked ravishing.

As she walked in the ballroom, she felt people looking at her. She was used to that and she did not pay attention, she was looking for her friend Lisa and her gentle husband Dr. Danz.

The place was magnificent as always. Lisa was a marvelous party maker. The Austrian crystal chandeliers only were breathtakingly dazzling, they were magical. Anataalie recognized many celebrities among the dancers.

Lisa was talking with an American actor, who was fairly successful in the film industry, and had a lot of promise. She was laughing.

Lisa was a comely person, of whom you could grow fond of almost immediately. She was always smiling and she had a profound artistic soul, she was a giver rather than a taker, and her heart was open to all.

She came running to Anataalie and said:
"I knew you would make it, my dear. I am so very happy Anataalie, the day would never have been complete without you, this Ball would have felt like an orphan."

The music was overwhelmingly ravishing, and soon Anataalie was no longer listening to the chatter of Lisa, but was focusing on the music.

All of a sudden, she felt herself been taken away on the dance floor and she heard Lisa saying:
"Have your first dance with my son."

Anataalie looked up and saw Lisa's son. Yes, he was a nice person too; a doctor married to an amazingly beautiful Polish piano player. He had showed her when he visited his parents in Dubai then, pictures of their wedding album.

He was a calm person, and as they danced, he told her that his father had been away on a business matter, urgent, and that he was here to replace him and keep all the guests at ease.

Anataalie said:
"But you should not fuss so much about me, you know, I am here only for the night. You better take care of your other invitees."

And so, Natalie walked away to the Buffet. She felt like eating some of the traditional Austrian food that she never could find in the Gulf.

As the Filipino maid helped her out, she felt a pair of eyes on her, and she looked up. It was the actor who had been talking to Lisa earlier.

He said:
"You are Anataalie, are you not?"

"Yes, and you are "Peter, replied Anataalie. I remember having seen the films in which you acted. You are quite talented."

"And so are you". replied Peter.

Anataalie looked sharply into his eyes and said:
"How do you know?"

"Does it matter?"

"No."

Anataalie continued, uncomfortable:
"It is a lovely ball, is not it?"

"Yes, it is even lovelier since you came here", Peter said intently.

Anataalie smiled:

"Yes, it is a phrase that has been told often, I can tell."

And she was putting down her plate, ready to leave the Buffet, when Peter said in a low voice:
"Please do not go"

Why?"
Anataalie was confused. He spoke so close to her. She asked: Why? What is the matter?"

Peter said:
"Forgive me Anataalie. I was not trying to flirt. I just said those words because I needed to talk to someone. Will you stay?"

There was so much pain in his eyes. Anataalie replied:
"Yes. But I think it would be best if we went into the dance floor, people may be wondering"

Peter said:
"As you wish. though I do not care about what others think or do not think."

"Fine", Anataalie said as she moved towards the dance floor, "This is a ball after all, we shall talk as we dance."

Peter was a handsome man, but Anataalie had seen so many handsome men. She was curious about the wild pain she had seen in the eyes of this actor.

She said:
"Go on Peter"

Peter said:
"Anataalie, please help me."

"Yes, if it is within my power, I will. What is it? "Anataalie probed again.

Peter started in a low voice:
"Well, Anataalie, Lisa, your friend and I are having an affair."

Anataalie felt cold in her heart, Dr.Danz and Lisa always presented the picture of the perfect couple. But yes, those things did happen. So she asked Peter:
"Yes? So?"

Peter continued:
"Well, Lisa is very much in love with me, and well how to put it. I am not in love with her. I am not even sure how I got there. She knows. I, on the other hand, am very much in love with her daughter and I want to marry her. I cannot think of my life without her.

Lisa found out and she had had a camera filming us in a hotel room and she is doing an emotional blackmail on me, warning me that if I did not go away from her she would reveal everything to her daughter."

Anataalie could not believe what she was hearing. As she looked away, she saw Lisa smiling at her. Were they talking about that Lisa, her friend she had known for years?

Peter continued:
"Tonight, you must help me. Because Lisa has fixed that business meeting for her husband away from the ballroom so that she can loosen the brakes of his car, and you know how icy the roads are. Tonight he

will come here, and she is planning to go home with her daughter and he will bring back the violin and other instruments in his car and drive alone home to meet them there.

The only thing being is that he will never get there, because the brakes would not function when he would have to take that steep turn on the way home. Please stop her, do something."

Anataalie said:
"But you, you must stop her, not me."

Peter said:
"If I interfere, cannot you see how so many lives will be ruined: hers, mine, her daughter's, and her husband's?

Anataalie became livid and thought: yes. What if he was right?

She said fine:
"Leave it to me. I will take care. Do not come close to me again tonight, she should not suspect anything."

And so Anataalie went to sit with others, and Lisa came to sit besides her, presenting her a wonderful cup of Austrian coffee.

Antaalie thanked Lisa. Lisa opened the conversation:
"I saw you dancing, what do you think of this actor? Oh he is a very fine actor and dancer, but we have met already."

Anataalie was thinking how to fix this problem very quickly, how to defuse the situation in the best way.

She said to Lisa:

"Well yes, Lisa, we are more than friends you know. We meet whenever we can."

Lisa was livid:
"How? Well you know how secretive I had always been about my private life. In fact, it was all because of him. He has a ugly affair with a married woman and he promised me that tonight everything would be sorted out."

Lisa hands were trembling. She said sharply:
"That is not a nice relationship Anataalie, this man is known to be a womanizer."

Anataalie felt the anguish, the stabs of pain in her friend's heart and she felt pain but she did not let it show.

She said:
" Yes, I know but he has changed a lot. He is true now. I am sure of it."

Lisa rose and said:
"Excuse me, Anataalie, my other guests."

"Well yes, of course, Lisa. Please attend your other guests. After all I came for him, I must be frank about it. Later he and I shall meet and plan for our future together."

Lisa went, she looked suddenly older, tired.

Anataalie loved Lisa, but there was no other way. She had to hurt her, before she self-destructed herself and her family.

Dr Danz had returned, and he showed up very gallantly at the ballroom, a charming man. The night went very well, and soon, Peter had left as the musicians. The Ball was over.

There was only Lisa, her daughter and Anataalie in the empty ballroom. Dr.Danz said:
"Tonight, it feels like our home back in Dubai. We were so happy there, do you remember?"

Anataalie replied, as she looked to Lisa:
"Yes, we are such good friends"

Lisa said:
"Yes, Anataalie it feels like Dubai and yet not totally. It is Salzburg, the city of the Viennese Ball, where everything ends with a crystal shoe."

Anataalie smiled to Lisa and said:
"How true your words sounds, I do feel like Cinderella, waiting to find her prince."

Lisa became livid, she fought to hide her tears. Then she said slowly:
"Wolfgang, I forgot to tell you. Your car is not in good order; there is something wrong with the brakes, so let us all go home in our daughter's car. Anataalie, we can drop you by your hotel if you wish."

Anataalie replied, relieved and anxious to please her friend:
"No, Lisa. I will go to my hotel room directly."

Lisa became very pale again and was trembling:
"To your hotel? Why do you not come to sleep at our home?"

Anataalie said:

"No, Lisa. All my things are at the hotel. It would make too much fuss to pick my things to go to your place and then my flight is tomorrow, very early morning."

Lisa said coldly:
"Yes, I do understand. Then I think we can wish you farewell now. Your schedule is always so tight."

Dr.Danz added:
"Yes Anataalie, next time, do stay longer. We enjoy your company so much, we miss you much here"

Anataalie looked at Dr. Danz and replied:
"Yes, I promise, next time, I will stay longer, yes."

All of a sudden, she realized that Dr.Danz had known of her wife's affair, of her intent of this evening. She read it in his eyes; she read the loud thank you in his eyes.
Lisa said:
"So let us have some apple strudel and some nice coffee, meanwhile the hotel staff will fix my violin and other stuff in our daughter 's car."

Dr.Danz looked at his wife lovingly and said:
"Lisa, what a wonderful idea. We all know that Anataalie loves Austrian Apple Strudel."

Lisa smiled:
"So there, let everyone relax, we shall have an Austrian strudel, and Anataalie we shall drop you at your hotel.""

Anataalie had found anew the Lisa she loved the woman she had known before the ugly revelations of Peter.

Lisa hurried to the buffet, and soon, the Filipino maid was pouring coffee to everyone, and Lisa was cutting the strudel and passing over the plates.

She came to sit down and handed over the plate of strudel to Anataalie and everyone enjoyed the togetherness in the empty ball-room, Dr Danz was telling jokes, Lisa was laughing and Anataalie enjoyed the new found warmth coming from this close knit family.

The night was over, and pretty soon, Dr Danz drove Anataalie up to the hotel, Lisa cried when Anataalie bade her good bye. She said:
"Lisa, you are far too sensitive, it is but a good bye you know."

Dr.Danz winked at Anataalie, they both knew that Lisa had a musician's heart, very fragile, she would cry easily…She was emotionally reactive to life.

And Anataalie saw the car drive away into the dusk.

She went to her hotel room. She did not know what to think. Perhaps Peter had exaggerated, or played an actor's prank on her. Maybe she had misread everyone's eyes. No, Lisa could never have intended to kill her husband. How? Dr. Danz was a wonderful man, well above the average by any standard. Such a kind and sophisticated man.

She decided that it had been nothing but a nightmare and fell asleep peacefully.

The next morning, the hotel maid entered as she had been told by Anataalie the next morning that her breakfast should be brought into the room and that she should be woken up early to catch her flight connection back to Dubai.

The maid called: "Madame."

There was no response.
No response would ever be made.
The hotel manager had just opened Anataalie's room. The hotel doctor had come and said:
"The young lady is dead, she has been poisoned by something she ate in the last 8 hours."

The hotel manager relaxed:
"He said she did not take any food or drink here since more than 15 hours."
-The End-

SHORT STORY 8

Madame Le Poete

The wind was blowing heavily in the cold winter night of London. The roads were empty. Occasionally, one lonely double deck bus would cruise the roads half-empty like a foggy contour ghost, its windows dimmed by an icy veil.

High up in a stately apartment suite building, Anataalie was sitting at her desk trying to write a letter to her mother, trying to find words kind to convey gently that she would be a bit delayed for Christmas, but that she would be in France for New Year.

Anataalie, was a young French artist and had been in London for almost a year now. She had been admitted in the famous St Martin School of Art. She was enjoying her time there, every student was so talented, the teachers were patient and helpful and she felt that every day was bringing her a new well of knowledge.

London was in its own right a trendy city when it came to art. Popular art was very much alive, and it could even be seen walking along the roads, when least expected. Yes indeed. Art did mix blatantly too with the traditional business suits and hats, and the orange robes of the Hare Krishna's bands that were very active this time of the year. It was hard to refuse to give some money to someone who went out in such light clothing. Suddenly someone passed by you that took your breath away long long white hair with mauve velvet dresses and a make up of glitters. It warmed the heart, like a sudden rainbow.

The street art was young and fun; the funk culture that missed nothing, from the pin in the nose to the hair tainted vibrant green, yellow, and red…

It was so much more refreshing in a way than the season fashions trends of Paris, which was rigorist and categorized. You had to be in, or you would not do.

Here, none really cared. London was unique in its laissez-faire attitude. Even Anataalie remembered a peculiar reaction to an event with a smile: recently there had been a fire in the Playboy Club, nothing grave but staff had to be evacuated immediately. All the bunny waitresses waited outside in their club outfit and… none looked back or stopped to have a glance at the beautiful girls. Ah, it would have been an entirely different story if this did happen in Paris or Milan.

Anataalie felt safe in her isolated place. The fireplace was glowing in the dim-lit room. It was a lovely room functional yet the carpet and tapestry on the walls gave it a warm look. On the mantle piece, there was a copper urn, and around its contours, the flames of the fireplace seem to do a magical dance.

Anataalie was wearing a long woolen home dress, light purple on which she had thrown a pure white shawl over her shoulder.

On her oak wood desk, there was a tall study lamp and a penholder, a tray with a sterling coffeepot, a creamer and a white and gold porcelain coffee cup.

She rested her hand around the cup absorbing the heat of the liquid through the lifelines of her hands. She was conversant with relaxation techniques; this was the easiest and her favorite too: wrapping her hands around something warm in times of stress.

Her hand seemed as fragile as the porcelain cup she was holding. Her face encased by her long chestnut hair was pale, milk and roses and her fawn eyes had a dreamy look about them, that always made you wonder whether she was truly following what you were telling her, whether she was listening at all. She seemed always near and yet so far away, unreachable.

Everything else was quiet, with a lingering mood of loneliness.

Anataalie had stayed inside for a week now, it was the holidays. Some of her student friends had dropped by, had come up to her door, they rang but she did not open that door. Anataalie was playing the exquisite game of being confined in her own magical and lonely island and so she was careful not to make a noise. She wanted everyone to think that she had left. And yes, she thought with inner pleasure and a sense of deep safety that everyone had assumed by now that she had left for France. Her phone was even disconnected.

Yes everyone she knew in London had by now believed that she had gone home for holidays, though her visitors left disappointed not to have had the opportunity to greet her before she left. People liked her so much at school and around where she lived or shopped or went.

She radiated a warm and discreet charisma. Anataalie at first appeared shy yet when one came closer one could grasp the decisiveness of her character. She was chic and friends liked to invite her out too. Her dress was always elegant yet very formal, like a barrier against others. People would stand a bit away from her in instinctive deference. She was a delicate and beautiful woman

And so on this winter night, Anataalie was writing on, as she had been doing so for nights now. She would work all through the night and sleep during the day. She felt a great inner pleasure in ignoring normal timings. Yet, she would observe that one rule "yea shall rest on the seventh day".

It was dark and she felt at peace, she stretched herself and went to the kitchen. Everything was immaculately clean and she went on to check on the food that she had in store. Yes, she would have to ration herself. Not much food was there, but it would do just fine, she was no great eater anyway. Well she could certainly live on biscuits and coffee; there was enough as for other things, well nevermind.

As she counted the biscuits, she realized that the sugar was over, and she had forgotten to replenish the stock. Well it was too late for that and yes, she would drink her coffee unsweetened.

She took a biscuit, broke it in too, and then pounded the other half into powder. She opened her window and put the powder in the icy windowpane. Soon sparrows came from the nest they made on the tree in front of the building and started singing and flying around.

Anataalie observed fascinated the sparrows taking the crumbs hurriedly and flying back to the nest to feed their young chicks. It was not before the 6 or 7th journey that the adult sparrows stayed on the pane and fed themselves in full view of Anataalie.

She had warmed some water and had put it in a small water bottle cap; she placed it besides the crumbs, the sparrows did not leave their spot, they did not mind Anataalie, and soon they drank the warm water, and bathed their wings hurriedly. Anataalie gently caressed the soft back of the sparrows. All was well with her special friends, and she closed the window on the winter night while the sparrows winged away to their nest.

The sparrows knew that every night there would be a treat for them.

Anataalie returned to the kitchen she had made a fresh pot of coffee and placed some more biscuits on the plate and she carried the tray all through the long corridor. She did not switch the light on so that the neighbors did not suspect that anyone was at home. She needed full and complete rest from the world. She felt an acute pleasure knowing that none knew of her existence. She felt as if she was the Outsider.

She went to the study room, and sat down again at her desk.

She continued writing all through the night, all in long hand, and pages after pages were filled with her inclined handwriting. At dusk, she stood up and went to take a silent shower, regulating the shower flow to be weak so that none would notice the sound in the pipes in the building she lived in.

She then put on her night clothes and without food went to sleep in the bunk-bed that she had kept for visitors in that same study room.

Six days had gone by in that fashion. The life of Anataalie had become very precisely planned so that all her energy was to be spent on her writing. She did not seem to be tired. Her resolve and speed of writing was the same.

Then three days before New Year, when dusk came again for her to leave her desk, she did not go to bed as usual. She plugged her PC and connected with British Airways. She reserved a seat, first class, London Paris for the next day. In twenty-four hours she would be at home to her family celebrating New Year. Everything had been packed earlier, presents and all.

Then she proceeded to connect to a new web address, the page on the screen was blank and demanded a password. She filled it in. The screen showed a message board and she proceeded to simply type in: Done. Collect tonight 3am.

After entering this message she switched off her PC.

She turned herself towards the mirror and thought it was time she pampered herself a bit. She took her beauty case, and started applying a seaweed beauty mask on her face, she checked her hands, did a manicure, applied hot oil to her hair, and in one hour, she was as beautiful as could be. She went to the kitchen and made some coffee, there was but one biscuit left. She smiled, yes her food management had been perfect, and she fed the birds half of that last biscuit and then herself with that last biscuit. Again she felt an acute pleasure in this minimalist feeding.

She went to sleep, relaxed. She dreamt of the nest and the birds, she felt at peace.

She woke up as usual, and got dressed as if for a dinner party. She had put a long ball gown and wore pearls. She looked ravishing.

She walked to the desk and proceeded to tie up her manuscript with a red ribbon. As she was done, she looked at the neat file and smiled; she was pleased with her work. It looked pretty, she liked it.

She sat in the sofa and casually returned to more mundane pursuits. She went through some Paris fashion Magazine. Yes she would buy some great clothes and matching bags and shoes and jewelry from Place Vendome, soon. She was vain, and loved beautiful things. She smiled. She loved to draw the attention when she walked into any room.

At 3am exactly of that same morning, there was a small knock at the door. Anataalie went quickly to open, an old lady entered. She kissed Anataalie on the cheek and waited until the door was closed to ask her in a low voice:
"How are you? Is it done?"

Anataalie replied:
"Madame Le Poete, my work is always done and perfectly done too."

She gave the manuscript to the old lady with gray hair. Madame Le Poete took a pair of glasses from her bag and said:
"Yes, Anataalie, your work has always been excellent and you have been paid in consequence."

Anataalie said:
"Yes, Madame, indeed, I was always paid as promised."

There was a silence as the old lady read quickly through the handwriting of Anataalie. The old lady said:

"None of this is recorded anywhere yes? It is not on your PC either, is it correct?"

Anataalie replied smiling:
"Well, yes. Why do you ask?"

The old lady said:
"Oh well, just to make sure. I am as thorough in my job as you are in your writing. Nice piece Anataalie, he will be very happy."

Anataalie said:
"When is he coming, Madame Le Poete?"

The old lady replied sharply:
"Not sure, you know we are not told such details"

Anataalie said:
"Of course".

The old lady rose and said:
"Anataalie, you are a wonderful writer, you are very talented. I must take leave of you now."

"Yes, Madame Le poete", of course" Anataalie replied as she rose.

As usual the old lady plunged one hand into her handbag, as she had done many times previously. She always paid Anataalie generously, and always put the bundles of the 100 Sterling Pounds notes in one scented envelope. She would do so again today.

Anataalie waited, Madame Le Poete was getting old. She felt affection for the old lady. Today she noticed how her hands trembled.

She remembered the first time she had met her at a poetic symposium in Turkey, they had told her she was 68, it was a year ago.

Madame Le Poete told Anataalie:
"Please let me kiss you farewell on this end of the year."

She pulled Anataalie towards her, and soon the limp body of Anataalie dropped to the floor, with blood oozing from her chest.

Madame Le poete kneeled in front of Anataalie. Anataalie was still breathing, and she smiled at Mme Le Poete, she seemed so happy. The old lady recoiled in fright and shock and recharged her silencer gun. She took all her courage and opened the mouth of Anataalie, and shot her again, mercilessly. This time the brain fragments flew in all directions. Madame Le Poete had quickly taken refuge behind the bathroom door. Only one or two drops of blood were on her bag, she cleaned them up with a piece of tissue.

And without a second look, she left.

Outside a black limousine was waiting. The driver opened the door, and she entered the car.

There was an oriental man. Madame Le Poete sat besides him and gave him the manuscript. He said:
"Is it any good? "

Madame Le Poete said:
"It is an excellent piece for the Peace conference. It is written in a wonderful purist French. It moved me to tears too."

Then the oriental man told the driver to stop at a gas station, as he felt starved. He said:

"Madame Le Poete, come you might use a cup of coffee."

She said in an exhausted voice:

"Yes, it is a good idea."

They went to the coffee shop and they had their coffee. As always Madame Le Poete asked to be excused and went to the ladies to repowder her face. This was a classic with her, he knew it. He followed her, and shot her 6 times, in the back, with his silencer. He checked: she was dead, he took her handbag and long coat and left by the back door.

He went quickly into the limousine, and he addressed the Chauffeur:

"Your Excellence, may now sit in the back seat, the job is done.

The peace conference shall be a success."

-The End-

Short Story 9

Do not tear the night sky

She stepped out of the Concorde at New York airport. The flight captain came out to wish her good bye; he took her hand and held it between his two hands for long minutes, looking into the eyes of the young departing passenger.

It was an unusual sight, everyone was looking at both of them because they were blocking the exit passage and delaying other passengers.

The young lady tore herself from this forced farewell and climbed down the aisle fast, and then she slowed and looked back over her shoulder, the captain was following her with his eyes, she waved. He smiled, and she heard him shouting: Anataalie, take good care, promise me, and disappeared in the cockpit of the airplane.

Anataalie was a young French woman, who had traveled often, she run her own company in the Arabian Gulf and she spent much time on international flight. She traveled light.

She cleared from the immigration counter fast, and collected her crocodile case and walked rapidly to the customs. She knew they would ask her to open her case, they always did. She came from so far away, and yet her suitcase was unusually light. The customer officer looked inside, to light and incredibly beautiful lace dress, one white and one black, with tiny velvet shoes of the same shade and returned a smile and say: have a nice stay Miss.

She smiled gently and walked away. He watched her as she went away. She was striking, tall slender with a pure satin skin, her fiery brown eyes under her long lashes contained a mystery yet to be elucidated, and her long auburn hair caught the morning sunlight.

She was wearing a mauve light travel suite of jersey, a pant and tunic, elegance without contours, and one could feel the beauty of her youth

A limousine from an East European country Embassy was waiting for her, and she disappeared in the crowd within the crowd.

It felt good to feel the morning breeze of New York, she kept the window slightly opened, and she breathed in deeply as she closed her eyes.

Only twenty-four hours ago, she had boarded a plane in Italy, Tuesday. She loved visiting Italy; she felt at ease there, life was busy and joyous. When in Italy she loved wearing either white or black.

She had stayed at friends, but she had to be in New York for important business meetings, and so she had boarded the first flight available Rome-New York.

It is amazing when she arrived at the airport, it looked rather desert, and there were but a few passengers. She was seated in the business class along with only 6 other passengers.

There were a few passengers in the economy class. As for the first class, three were people, but that area had not been opened, and the flight took off fairly quickly.

Soon, the captain voice came through informing that the flight was on schedule. Yes, the plane was on its way, flying like an eagle through the night.

Anataalie closed her eyes, she could make out any longer when was really the time of night or day, she traveled through so many lands, and different calendars, that she just followed her own body clock, all she needed to recharge herself was to be totally alone for a few hours, and it was as good as any long night sleep.

Anataalie felt safe, she seldom felt that way any more. The stewardess was a young American lady, with countryside feel about her, she asked Natalie if she would like a blanket or something warm to drink.

Anataalie thanked her; she only wanted to find some peace in that temporary shelter of an aircraft flying through the night.

None would disturb her. The other few passengers in the business class were all aged people, also grabbing a nap in that night, as she did. Everything was silent and safe.

An hour had passed; Anataalie was asleep when a young woman run through the business class, forcing her way through the first class section. creating a commotion close to Anataalie

All went very quickly, the stewardess came barring the entrance to the first class section with her body, and the woman did not say a word, she had a knife in her hand, and just slashed the face of the stewardess.

Blood gushed with a fresh metallic scent from the wound.

Anataalie jumped on her feet, and disengaged the stewardess from the fight, took her way, and immediately, took one of the napkins, and pressed it hard to the face of the stewardess who was under shock and crying.

The aggressor had followed back Anataalie and the stewardess, and was standing there with her bloodied knife and she was smiling triumphantly. Anataalie did not pay attention to her, she knew that it is best to look away from insane and aggressive people.

She just eyed her shortly to gauge as to how dangerous and insane that woman was. She was a short and stocky black woman, her face revealed that she was common and vulgar. And Anataalie knew at that time that that type of people was the worst, and she was to be feared and controlled. The sooner the better.

A man in dark suit came out from the first class along with the captain and asked the woman:
"Who are you? Why are you doing this? You must be tired, let us give you something to relax".
As they attempted to come close to the woman, she took from inside her jacket a gun, and said:
Do not come closer to me, I rule here, do you hear me, and that is for disturbing my peace.

She cruelly tore the towel from the stewardess's injured face, and slashed it again, fast. So fast, that Anataalie was shocked and dazed by the cruelty of that act.

Anataalie raised and pushed as hard as she could in the stomach of the woman, who lost her balance and fell on the floor. But the woman was quicker than a tiger, she jumped back to her feet and just fired at the man in black suit, he collapsed, and fragments of his blasted brain went to sully the panels of the aircraft.

Anataalie was tending to the stewardess and putting cold water on the twice injured face, and she took one of the pillow and was talking to the stewardess, telling her to keep the pillow over her head, as a protection against further attacks.

Anataalie raised her gaze and saw for the first time the Captain, he was an American man of 50, his face was livid, and he was pulling the dead body of the passenger, covering it up with a blanket.

People were screaming, and he urged everyone to stay calm. Somehow their eyes met and they knew they would draw courage and energy from each other. They had hardly met, but they already knew that they would face this together to protect the plane, the crews and the passengers

From the economy class, two men came and joined the women; they were laughing, and greeting the woman:

"Nice work Mary Dread, nuff respect to you.

The woman smiled, and Anataalie noticed how girlish she looked.

The problem had just started.
The captain asked:
"What is it that you want. Please make your demands, and do not mess on my flight.

One of the man hit the captain face with his fist and shouted:
"Shut up, we talk you listen. We shall burn the white liars….

Anataalie recognized the accent in the word 'bun"…. She had heard it earlier; it was a primitive pronunciation, the one that came with the illusion of the Mental Slavery.

The captain did not emit a word or a noise that he had felt pain, he stood as if nothing had happened, and his lower jaw was red. He looked at Anataalie and she knew he was strong.

But what did they want? She was tending to the stewardess who was hurting, the blood has stopped burping from the wounds, but she was crying out of panic.

Mary Dread, she stocky short woman hated her, she kept looking at her, calling her: white witch to bun…Anataalie did not reply.

Then she lost interest, and they went into the first class. As they entered, Anataalie heard the gun being fired several times, and the captain went in, she followed. Their fate was tied.

In a seat besides the window was sited an old man with a skullcap on his head, a long robe of purple velour. He was so frail, and luminescent. Bodies of men in dark suits were thrown on one side, and Anataalie noticed that they all were wearing around their neck the cross of Jesus Christ.

The old man too…Anatalie looked at the captain with total amazement and asked: The Pope? The captain nodded his head.

Yes, it was the Pope. Anataalie came closer and the elderly man did not have any fear, inspite of the priest killed in front of him, it was impossible to read in his face what he was feeling. He was enveloped by a spiritual light so profound that ordinary logic was of no use here.

He was praying, he felt so far away from the plane.

The gang was laughing: three armed with guns, knives and grenades. They taunted him and said:
"You are a fraud". Only the Lion Heart is the light, and it is black.

You are not black; you lied to the world.

The Pope replied with a voice gentle and soft:
Be well, my children, I forgive you.

Mary Dread was furious and said:
Listen Brethren, he calls us his children, and we are not your children, imposter, the Children of Jah. You and your Church have fabricated the biggest lie of the universe, the Christ.

And she took her knife and attempted to slash the face of the Pope, somehow he raised his eyes and lock his gaze to her gaze and she got startled, stopped in her attack and withdrew behind the men. The men were lost for a while, but they decided of a common accord to slap the face of the Pope. They did so, and not a nerve in the pope's face moved. They tore off the cross from the chest of the Pope, and Anataalie felt as if a light has been switched off, the face of the elderly men showed no sign of fright, it became extinguished.

At that point, the co-pilot had received permission to land in Heathrow Airport, the gang wanted food and money, and they agreed to let everyone go except for the captain and his co-pilot, Anataalie and the Pope. The captain argued and said why do you want the woman to stay here?

They shouted:
Do not cheat us, she is a spy, we know that kind, she is a white witch, she will burn in hell, with you all, as the Lion looks on.

In half an hour, the food and the money was sent in, and the rest of the passengers evacuated, the air hostess cried again as she left Anataalie. Anataalie reassured her:
I will be fine, we shall meet in New York, later, and we shall meet, and go quickly…

The gang refused to let the dead bodies be evacuated, or moved.

So the frail old man was ordered to go and sit with Anataalie in the Business Class.
The short and stocky woman was eating noisily, telling cruelly:
" You are going to die, there is no need to feed you"

Anataalie did not reply. The elderly man was deep in spiritual meditation as if he was not of this world any longer. The captain kept close to the old man, guarding him in a way with his strong body.

Anataalie felt anger, and so she started to sing:
No woman No cry…

The gang was lost, mesmerized by the voice of Anataalie.

The captain looked into Anataalie's eyes; he was struck by the strong magnetism of her gaze. He only understood her deep anger; she resented deeply that the old man was made a prisoner. He understood too that the old man was too frail, another blow and he would not make it through this night.

She sang and they were hypnotized. At the end, she said:
Do no tear the night sky…

And the stocky woman laughed hysterically, she insulted the Pope.

The Pope was so frail, so luminous. She did not understand why people would want to harm him; after all he was only the keeper of the balance between good and evil.

The gang understood the anger of Anataalie; one of the men approached the frail man and slapped him again. The Pope did not react…but Anataalie felt the soul of the frail man starting to take leave of his mortal cloak. Anataalie said: Not yet, do tear the night sky.

Then all of a sudden the plane went through a turbulent zone; the plane was shaking and was not finding its course. There was more commotion in the plane. The frail old man did not move, did not seem to care. The gang shouted at the captain to go and put things right.

The captain did so.

Something, extraordinary was happening, the aircraft seemed to have stopped in the night sky, the windows and doors of the aircraft were open by some unseen force, the frail man went in the middle of the aisle and knelt down praying silently.

The aircraft was totally immobile, a cold light came into the aircraft, and the three were shivering. Anataalie understood the cold but did not feel it, the captain and his pilot were dazed, slowly they went into a hypnotic coma.

Then suddenly a rain of nails fell on the aircraft; the alley was a carpeted sharp nail.

The gang was shivering with fear, they feared the pain that the nails brought along, and the fear they now felt for their life and their death.

The frail man was still praying, he tried to rise, he was too frail, Anataalie felt herself walking on the nail barefoot, she felt no pain, the nails did not hurt her, and she reached to the old man and tended to him.

The gang seeing this tried to follow Anataalie and get to the old frail man, but as they advanced, the nails had pierced their shoes and had hurt the sole of their feet, they cried in agony.

The short woman took her gun and aimed slowly towards Anataalie, Anataalie did not move and said:
You are a fool, try and bun me now.
You are fools

Can you not understand? You have come here and claimed a life of a messenger to be a lie, when you are nothing that clay.

He was made of clay to come and help humanity, even that clay you want for yourself, there it is, a rain of nails, feel them as he did, they are all yours.

Another gush of wind came, and in a split of a second took away the mantle of nails and the gang that has cloaked it with.

Then, the plane was back on course, the voice of the pilot could be heard: Captain we are arriving to New York Airport.

The captain came out of his trance, and looked around there were none but himself, Anataalie and the Pope.

The captain did not ask any question, he looked into Anataalie's eyes and he knew that he did not need to know what happened. His soul was tranquil.

On their arrival, the Pope was taken away, and the tour went well…he said that Tuesday would never come.

The captain went to his headquarters to give a full description of the gang to help to apprehend them wherever they would show up again…

…And Anataalie walked in a business meeting. The secretary asked her:
How was your flight, Mademoiselle Anataalie"

"Fine, Grace, just fine, thank you…

The meeting started.

-The End-

SHORT STORY 10

The Hakim : The Egyptian Judge's own life sentence

The courtroom was stuffy in a small town in the south of Egypt. Abdullah, the Qadi/hakim, as he was called, had been born in a prosperous family, his fathers, grandfathers; ancestors were all men of law.

His great grand father dispensed his rulings under the palm tree next to the house that he had built with his own two hands. As in those times, to be selected as a judge was paid by deep respect and small gifts, never by a wage. It was a question of honor, the honor of the being the chosen one to keep the life of the village in good order.

Since then, of course, the family had prospered and Abdullah had been sent to Paris to study law at La Sorbonne, he had obtained his Ph.D. there, and when his studies were over he came back home to Egypt to work for the Ministry of Justice- Ozarat al—Moahaqamat. At first, because of his young age, he was put to review laws and prepare the court files. He was twenty-five and had lofty ideas on how law should be applied.

After all in Paris, he used to spend evenings comparing notes with the other students of La Sorbonne, he spent days sitting in tribunals, watching verdicts given then and there.

He visited jails and reviewed files of inmates who were lodging appeals against set judgments, he always felt the thrill that justice was indeed a matter of interpretation, and he had developed that special finesse in judgement that made him soon a brilliant student, known well to his professors for his zeal in getting to the bottom of things as they put it.

Going back to Egypt felt good to his heart, he had missed his family and his aging father very much.

But soon, he realized that life and the textbooks of Paris were so much more different from the life situation he witnessed here than he had anticipated.

People were poor; courtrooms were places that were looked down upon, while he was looked up as some kind of deity, set apart in rigidity. He felt cold there in his heart.

He got set in his ways, and soon as it had been decided almost on the day he was born, that he would marry Noura his cousin by blood. She was a very pious lady, and she bore him four strong children, as he slowly climbed the scale in his profession and was given the highest position of Head Hakim of the bigger city nearby.

That was a major transition, and he soon bought a large house, a detached villa with boundaries, a marble construction, very luxurious with chandeliers and stairs covered with Turkish carpets, imported antiques. They had servants, in uniforms, and a driver to take the children to school.

He had reached the climax of his career, and he was now among the top new bourgeois of Egypt.

But as life went on, he realized his power, his agility his finesse and zeal at passing rulings and judgement were really unused to their full potentials. He was highly respected, but he felt disdain for the people that came before him, most were poor, ignorant, their cases were repetitive and boring: divorce cases, inheritance disputes, land disputes.

Soon he went to the courtroom without much enthusiasm; he was tired of the routine. But he had made his life there and he had reached the highest position at a very young age indeed: 45 years.

As his interest for his professional life declined, he found himself more and more drawn to the artistic life of Egypt, and so he started to frequent art gallery openings, soirees. His spouse would sometimes accompany him, but she was a homely lady, and she was happy to stay home surrounded by her children and servants.

So he went alone, and he felt lonely.

Soon the soirees got longer, he went to night clubs when he felt the painful void in his soul, something was missing though he did not quite understand what it was, but he had been missing.

The longing in him felt like a deep pain, he could not define the ache, he had everything a man could possibly want.

Then one night he entered a smaller nightclub and lazily watched the belly dancers routine, he was used to that too, it did not hold much attraction anymore, but he had nothing better to do, the movement, the loud music, the smoke distracted him from his inner pain.

Then Halla came on stage and danced on the music of Abdul Wahab…She was different, she was totally covered with a dark green silk suit, and she was devoid of glitter, of jewelry. Halla was an enigma made up only by her dance the music and her long silky hair. When her dance was finished, she would go away, she did not seem to care for the dollars that were thrown over her as she danced… she just vanished.

The Hakim was intrigued, none heard her voice, she was close and yet so far away, none would tell him about her, because none really knew her or cared to know her. There were other dancers, always new others, the public was unfaithful.

He had become fascinated by her dance, which never seemed to be the same and yet was never also totally different from the previous evenings. Far and so close: he did not which of the two would describe her, really

For months, he went every night to the same place, he could get no closer no matter how hard he tried to be noticed, he would order for flowers, throw dollars on the stage, orders for dozens of the most expensive French Champagne bottles to be placed around her as she danced.

He asked to talk to her, she would never come.

Then he stopped going to the nightclub for a week but he realized that the void in his soul had been partially filled by her. He was lost; he did not comprehend it.

Why? How?

He could not bear to stay away from that place, so he went again for months, he got no closer, but he felt less lonely during the days. He felt kinder towards the cases that were brought to him.

Then one day, as his driver slowed down due to heavy traffic congestion, on the way to the courtroom, he saw her in the market. At once he recognized her walk and hair…He jumped out of the car and called:

"Halla".

She turned and smiled:
Yes Abdullah?"

He said:
"Halla, I come to watch you dancing every night"

She replied softly:
"Yes Hakim I know that."

The Hakim went on:
" Why do you not want to talk to me there? "

She said:
" No, I could not, it is not so polite you know. "

Startled by her replied, he muttered
"But…"

She interrupted him:

"Yes, I dance, but that is all. I have 9 brothers and sisters, and my father is very ill, there is no other way for us"

He said
"Can I meet you again?"

Halla smiled gently:
"No, this would not be considered polite. You see this is where I live" as she pointed out to her dwelling.

And he saw the poor Egyptian building, the poverty…he understood…

His soul opened then and there, as it used to while he was in Paris, when everything was still possible. The light entered in his heart.

He said:
"Halla, I will see your father, as I want to marry you"

She lowered her eyes:
"Do as you wish Hakim"

Abdullah went home and called his wife in his study and told her.

He was the Hakim and he passed the ruling then and there, he decided what was fair.
His wife did not raise any objection none did, he was the Hakim.

And so one month later, Halla and he moved into a smaller house, a nice house like a tiny French bangalow.

She did not go to dance anymore, and she now wore the veil and the abbayah.

He stopped going out in the evening, and started to love his work.

In every case, he saw the father, the mother of Halla, in every woman, he discovered a new facet of the diamond of life. He became involved, caring, concerned.

The absence of Halla in the nightclub was explained curtly, she had found a rich suitor who paid her heavily to wear the veil and renounce her art. It was even mentioned in the newspapers of Cairo

But Halla is known now as the wife of the Hakim, and no rumors reach her, and that place where her husband passes his ruling is a joyous and simple place, like his life…the void of his soul has been filled by the prayers that calls on him five times a day and to which he truly respond…There lies the truth of the Hakim and of Halla, his second and last wife.

They did never travel outside of Egypt for their honeymoon or vacation. She did never wear any ornaments, but on her there is a special glow, the glow of true happiness, and now children fill the house with laughter…Halla and the Hakim's children…they walk to school and the greatest Hakim of Egypt walks to the courtroom and Halla cooks the meals…

There is the ruling of the Greatest Hakim of Egypt, his own life sentence: the highest in rank shall walk to the courtroom to protect the poor and the rich alike…in simplicity and in truth.

-The End-

Short Story 11

The Prostration Mark

It was very hot, on the roads of Dubai road; he kept drying the sweat from his face with a dirty towel. A taxi-driver of 40 years old dressed in the pathan ethnic loose outfit a baggy brown cotton trouser and a loose shirt to the knees made of brown cotton…. His shirt was soaked with sweat.

It was 50 degrees and the air-cooling in his old taxi was not working very well.

The passenger on the seat behind, a tall man dressed in a designer suit, kept complaining:
"Hey! Why is your air-conditioning not working?
Akbar laughed and said:
"It is working, the sun is very very hot, and none can cool it"
And he smiled a happy smile.

His face was open, he wore the Muslim cap on his head and wore the beard too, there was a dark spot on his forehead, the spot where his skin touches the grounds, in prostration while praying, every day five times, anywhere he could be, in the mosque, or on the pavement…the Muslim prayer is not limited within walls, it flies free, it is equal for the poor and the rich, the ruler and the ruled.

Akbar cleansed away again the sweat from his face, with the towel, and when it touched this dark and roughened prostration mark on his forehead, he smiled again. He remembered that last Friday when he went to the main mosque with his sons and brothers…. They had taken a bath and had put on sweet fragrances from Arabia. Guards all praying there flanked the ruler together: there was no partition…. When the prayer was over, the ruler proceeded to leave but on his way out, everyone stood a bit away to show respect. That Friday the ruler somehow stopped by Akbar and his sons and gave him his hand and greeted him with a gentle smile and uttered a verse (Aayat):

"And this is a book which we have revealed (is) a blessing: so follow it and be righteous…."

All others accompanied the ruler's words and completed the Aayat

"That ye may receive mercy…"

Everyone spoke about it in his neighborhood that Akbar was given an accolade by the ruler…Akbar did not feel proud just thankful because he knows that this accolade on a Friday prayer was the accolade of a brother to another brother…. There was no expectation or desire in this greeting. Still he made his heart swell with love.

That Friday had been a great day at home, they spread the carpet on the floor and his wife brought the food for the men, everything was laid nicely on the carpet and all of them sat on the floor eating with their hands.

The women ate in another room. laughing and singing.

During that time, Akbar forgot all about his hardships, the fact that he drove his taxi some 18 hours a day, earning just enough to feed his family, and pay his sponsor to allow him to drive the taxi legally.

The work was hard but it fed his family, it was enough. At time fear came in his heart for a while at the though that his son was still young and should anything happen to him, his family would be destitute. But then the words came to him and he recited the aayat and went to pray.

The passenger was edgy and rude, he kept saying:
" Hurry, it is hot, hurry it is hot."
Each time he smiled and re-iterated:
"Sir, be patient, I cannot over-speed it is against the law."

To make pass the time, he put some music on, the passenger rudely asked him to switch off the silly music and drive, and drive...Akbar said:
"As you want brother"
He could see the harsh face of the suited man in the mirror. He thought to himself: I may be a poor man, I may not have a suit, but I would not like to look like him: his face is so hostile...and he recited the aayat.

Meanwhile the passenger told him,
"Stop here. How much?
Akbar said:
"Twenty Five dirhams, please"

The passenger shouted:
"No, you will get Ten Dirhams"
Akbar said:
"This is not good but go I do not want your money".

Akbar's day went on, he got some more passengers, and in the evening at 12 midnight he drove home. He parked his taxi in its usual place. His eldest son came out to help him clean the inside of the taxi.

As Akbar was checking the oil, the water level of the taxi, so that in the morning he could start his day placidly, his son called:
"Father, look I found a bag."

Akbar said:
"Son, show me."
As they opened the bag, they found 100,000USD as well as some id papers, yes it was that rude passenger.

Akbar said:
"No time to eat or to sleep, let me go to the police station and hand over the bag without delay, that man may be stranded due to lack of money."

Akbar went to the station: the police officer did not look at him and Akbar had to wait until the officer did find time for him. He said:
"What is it you want, Pathan?"
He said:
"I am a taxi driver and I found this bag in my taxi, one hundred thousand dollars."
At once the police officer called his major and all the details were taken.

They told Akbar to go home.

Late at night, there was a knock at his doors very loud, a police officer called:
"Is this the place of Akbar?"
Akbar came out and said:
"Yes, it is, and I am Akbar"
To his utmost dismay they caught him and put menacles on his hands, and said:
"You are under arrest."

He was so dazed, what happened he said. The Police Officers said we do not know we have an arrest warrant with your name on it.

As he was taken to the police station, the colonel came out and said:
"Yes you did bring us that money but meanwhile one sultan lodged a complaint that as on his way to the bank he was robbed of the money."

Akbar felt doomed. That man did this to him.
He said:
"But I am telling you.
He pleaded, the colonel said:
"There is nothing we can say now, and it is a criminal offence the judge will deal with you. "
He said:
"But I did not do it…"

This Friday, as Akbar was still languishing in jail, all his brothers and sons went to the Grand Mosque.

Again. As the ruler made his way out he looked on the group and asked the son
"Where is your father, why has he not come to the Grand Mosque? It is Friday…The son cried and said:
"Oh Ruler, they have arrested my father."

The Ruler said:
"Enough son, come to my office tomorrow morning, tell the security guard your name, you will be let in."

The son was let in the next morning into the ruler's office, a most magnificent place. Between tears the son recollected the plight of his father.

The ruler called his private secretary and said
" Go tell the colonel to come here with the file, meanwhile send some dates to Akbar in his cell."

The colonel came with the file. The ruler's face was very dark and the colonel was shaking.

He asked the boy:
"When did you find that money? "

The boy replied:
"On Saturday night, Esteemed Ruler."

Then the Ruler asked the colonel:
"When was a complaint lodged for theft of that amount?"

"Friday noon", answered the Colonel
The ruler said:
"The complainant is a very bad man, because I am the witness to Akbar, I was praying with him at the Grand Mosque. Rush and go free Akbar and do your duty colonel, for today is your last day in my employ. Arrest this man, as he is now the cause of your misery, and you were the cause to a stain on a good man's name due to your laziness."
Justice is done."

As he recited the aayat:

".... And when yea judge between man and man, that you judge with justice…"

-The End-

SHORT STORY 12

Dying of Peace

A blizzard had been blowing over that ghostly town for days now, it was almost hard to recognize the lay of the land and find the way back to the houses.

Anataalie had been walking for hours in the snowy desert. It was taking all the strength of her twenty-five years to move on, the icy wind seemed to be forcibly taking her waist in a bid to immobilize her and root her in a desolate death.

But she was strong, she had decided that she would make it, that she would return.

She finally reached the nearest shop.

It was a dark room, filled with spider webs; she could hear the sound of rats moving underneath the rotting wooden parquet. The shop's shelves were all bare except for some dry lentils bags, she took them all. She knew that the village was as empty as the shop she just left, not even oil to light the night lamps, and that she would waste precious time and energy looking any further.

But she made another attempt and crossed over to the village tavern: there too there was nothing at all left except for some dark and bitter chocolate bars, a dozen, she bought them all as well and paid with one of her jewelry pieces, even though she knew there were no living soul there claiming for payment.

Her way back was arduous; it took all of her strength. The road was not safe at all; branches were falling off the trees under the sheer weight of the frost and snow. She felt so anxious, she could feel beneath her warm cloak the sweat running down her spine…But soon she reached the barrack she now called home.

As she entered, and the door cringed, she saw them all sitting by the fire place, lifting their faces towards her, offering their broken-biscuit smiles. They had almost no teeth in their thin lipped mouths which kept on narrating to each other tales of their youth.

All of the inhabitants of the barrack were over eighty years old. Anataalie was the only person with youth.

They shrieked with pleasure at seeing her coming back safe, and with bags in her arms. One of the elder men took upon himself to ask questions on behalf of the others:

"Miss Anataalie, you have done so much for us already. We understand that this is getting more difficult day after day. How can we all be kept alive? Some of us could leave for the benefit of the others and."

"…Stop it, right now! "Anataalie interrupted sharply.

In her heart, she knew that was the last gulag of times, they were stuck with Peace, as War has flown away to further skies with the Overmen.

They had no use for peace and wisdom and old people, the one who had no strength to engage in warfare. They had to walk back to the beginning of Time and truly find Him again.

The rest of Humanity as old and weak as it was now on earth would not be divided; she would not allow it. No more burning towers and despair blown in junks of bloody flesh all over the market place. No more.

She smiled, and informed that they would have their Last Supper: all the lentils and the chocolate would nourish them, as they had not been for a while. Tonight the hungry mouth of man would be fed, yes.

When night came, and each one of them was full with nourishment, a deafening sound from the sky came. The all came out and they saw the unbelievable, the OverMan had destroyed the stars and the moon.

Anataalie looked at them as they nodded their heads.

She sat at her old piano and played the Swan Lake.

Each one of them stood at the brim of that unique humanity tear, and jumped deep and slow in the Eternal.

When the last key had been played, Anataalie followed the last suicide of humankind in her final show of support.

It was the seventh day from Creation, nothing would be replicated and her soul would rest in truth.

- The End-

Short Story 13

The Sea Cruise

Cannes, of France, was vibrant in this time of the year, all the would be or should be celebrities were there, looking around to meet one of the famous films stars they have heard were living in Cannes. Yet, all of those stars had left and most migrated to Beverly Hills in America where privacy was more protected than it was in France.

The French has always had a peculiar philosophical approach about the privacy of a beautiful woman. They would say: so what, she is beautiful, it is normal that people want to look at her. Brigitte Bardot had tried what the Pharos of Egypt had failed to achieve, to put a boundary wall around her small area of the sea beach. She wanted to fence her piece of quiet and tranquility, to no avail. She too had moved away.

But people of all kinds still believed in the legend of Cannes, and that they would meet a famous person who would change their lives forever. And it was getting more and more crowded as time came closer to June

Many luxury cruisers were lining the shores of Cannes. And there was a brand new cruiser called NE ME QUITTE PAS, in English IF YOU GO AWAY. Yes, the cruiser has been named as per the song title of

Jacques Brel, the solitary man of France who gave a rendezvous with his death on the sea waves.

A young woman was standing near NE Me Quitte Pas, her name was Anataalie. Her hair was shining in the sun; they look like warm copper. She looked like an actress or a model, one could tell by the way she sported her white suit. She simply looked stunning and passers-by would take photographs of her. Some said she was the sister of Jacqueline Onassis. Anataalie did not mind the cameras; she was used to them.

As she was looking at the brand new cruiser, a Mercedes pulled down and a driver opened the back door. Yusuf has arrived. He looked so different when dressed with western casual and chic clothing, than he did when he wore the local dishdasha of the Arabian Gulf. Yusuf was a Kuwaiti business tycoon, immensely wealthy. He smiled as he scrutinized his new purchase. Yes, he liked the cruiser. He was a connoisseur. His family had been traders for ages; they had owned fleets of ships. He narrated often, while among close friends, how his great great grandfathers took the Dow (Arabian wooden boats) to sell their harvest of pearls to the orient and Africa... He had his own pleasure boats too back in Kuwait.

In Europe things were freer, convention was not so rigid and the look of anticipation was on his face. He was indeed looking forward to man his own luxury cruiser with a few helpers. He was anxious to use his hands.

He was an intelligent man, a self-reliant man, and Yusuf stopped for a while then went on the bridge and boarded his cruiser. He had closed the deal only last week, and named it after a song that Aantaalie had explained to him in great details, and what the words really meant to the French soul. Ne Me Quitte Pas.

Anataalie waited outside, she knew Yusuf to be very independent and proud. She offered no help or explanation. Within a few minutes, Yusuf came out and said everything is fine.

He said to Anataalie:
"Now, please advise our invitees that they should be on board soonest, as we are ready to sail away tonight."

Antaalie smiled.

Yusuf had already gone back into the Mercedes, and Anataalie went back to her hotel. Sufficient stocks for a week were being brought onto the cruiser; there were three helpers supervising the task.

She went back to the Meridien Hotel, and rang each room of Yusuf's invitees informing them to get going and that the cruise was on. None of those people Anataalie or Yousuf had met before… Yusuf has arbitrarily, Anataalie recalled, looked under a list in an association for retired seamen. He had made his choice quickly and chose six couples: four couples out of the six were black American; one was Native American, and the last plain American (of Irish origin). Those people were thrilled when they heard the news. They felt as if they had won the lottery. They did not know much more, but the next day, each received a bouquet of flowers with their hotels reservations tickets.

And so that evening, all of them boarded the cruiser, with great excitement. It was midnight, and Yusuf came the same way he had earlier in the morning, he was wearing a light white suit and soft-shoes, and a captain hat, and without saying a word, he boarded the cruiser. Anataalie was on board already looking ahead at the sea.

Yusuf stayed behind giving a last look to the land he had just left, and then he turned towards Anataalie with a deep look in his eyes and said to Anataalie:

"Please see to the guests, and we shall sail right away."

The sea was calm and Yousuf enjoyed sailing the cruiser, the sea was beautiful, and the breeze was energizing.

Then at 3am, the helpers took over, and Yusuf came down to the dining room. Everything was splendid, the food, the table was magnificent. Everyone had obviously dressed up, and when Yusuf entered, everyone rose. Yusuf smiled and said:

"Well I am only a temporary captain, so let us assume there are no ranks here and let us enjoy ourselves as among good friends."

This was enough to immediately relax the atmosphere.

The Native American couple said:
"It is so beautiful. "

The lady, a short and plump lady with long and lustrous hair said:

"Did you know that I had never gone to the sea before. Is not it absurd? My own husband was in the navy for most of his life, but well I never made it to the sea, until now that is."

She shook her head pensively and added quickly:

"Well, you know how it is, things are pretty expensive…"

And the she talked of the Native American land, the trails of their ancestors, how she took strength in the old ways while her husband was away.

Anataalie said:

"Yes, I had a friend once, a great soul from the Cherokee Tribe. He passed away last spring"

The lady was so happy. Yet all of a sudden, her face became grave she said: "During one of those times when my husband was away, I asked my elder son to take our old car from the garage, and he was shot eight times in the back, just to steal that old car, an old car. Oh my son!"

She cried softly, blowing her nose in the napkin as, her husband put her arms around her and said:

"Do not cry, woman, our son is well, he is with our elders in the native land of the soul."

Yousuf took the plate of the Native American lady and said:
"Eat, lady, this food cannot be wasted. Food should not be wasted."
She looked up and smiled through her tears:
" Yes, you are absolutely correct. Thank you so much sir, it means a lot to me to have been able to be on the sea with my husband."

Anataalie smiled as she touched the lady's hand:
"Yes, of course. And later, you can go and sit on the deck; it is so beautiful…. The sea at night is unforgettable."

The evening went quite well and everyone was up till 5am, they went up to deck and enjoyed the rest of the night, drinking tea and coffee, chatting away.

Then quietly, Anataalie went close to the Native American couple and said:

"We shall touch land shortly, the next port is an hour away." She added: "Mr. Yousuf wants you to disembark then."

The Native American man was surprised:

"Did we do something to displease him? If so we apologize, he seems such a good man, such a decent chap, maybe we should have not talked about our sadness, people do not want to hear sad news, they always need to laugh and be merry"

His wife was bewildered, and started crying.

Anataalie interrupted promptly:

"No, you did not offend the host in any manner. Please, Mr. Yusuf is a complex person, but he did enjoy your company a lot. In fact he asked me to present you this envelope. In it you will find a check to pay off the mortgage on your house and you shall be paid 5000USD a month for the remainder of your life. Your trip back home has been arranged. Please do not say a thing to anyone, do not thank Mr. Yousuf, he does not like emotional displays. "

They were shocked yet beaming with joy, they felt so relieved so happy…the lady was crying again. Anataalie came close to her and said:

"And this madam is from me. "

She gave a small Cherokee leather pouch in which was a tiny tortoise brooch in pure gold and emeralds. The lady did not know what to say she kissed Anataalie on both cheeks. Anataalie laughed but reminded them:

"Now you must get ready to disembark, does not say a thing to anyone."

On the second day, Yusuf did not steer the cruiser; he was a bit weary. He said he had got a cold. But he was going to appear in the evening on the deck where a sea fish barbecue would be taking place.

The Native American couple had left, and people were told they had to go home on emergency. None raised anymore questions. None really cared. The guests were so much enjoying their trip to waste time on questions: their rooms were like royal suites and they were indeed treated like royalties.

At night, everyone came on deck, the barbecue party was a success and the helper had brought up from Yusuf's rooms, an old record player an antique piece, and soon the air was filled with Armstrong's songs. The black Americans were very happy, they felt at home, the way it used to be in Louisiana, and they talked of their heritage. Yusuf was particularly anxious to hear about their lives. He asked many questions and the guests were happy to respond. Yusuf explained that his ancestors had traded often with Africa. His own grandfather told him how kind Africans were to him. He recalled one story of his grandfather where he explained how one of his boat's mates was saved by a villager, a tiger had attacked him…He lost a limb but he made it. I have been narrated this story so many times, Yusuf said:
"I feel sad about the racial tensions in the world really."

The guests said:
"Well we do too, because we went to fight for a country that we were told was ours, our blood was shed…yet when we came home, we found nothing but contempt and racism. Our children are not allowed to do so well in school. We are so worried about our children's future, it feels so bleak even now."

It had been a great night, but Yusuf felt very tired. And so at 5am, Yusuf took leave and joked on how they were living like in the Arabian nights: exchanging tales during the night and sleeping the day away.... Everyone laughed.

The white couple left soon after as they felt a bit left out, the three black skin couples had bonded and had become very close friends over the last two nights on the sea.... And so as the dawn was coming, Anataalie approached them. She said:

"Well take this as confidential, Yusuf has been touched by your tales, and he has asked me to tell you that every month each couple among you shall received 5,000USD and any expenses related to the education of your existing children of which I have a list shall be fully be paid for. Yusuf wish them to go as high as Ph.D. degree and make him proud."

The couples were baffled, but their exuberant nature took over and they started dancing on Armstrong records on the deck. Anataalie gave them each an envelope and told them to disembark, as the cruiser was touching land within ten minutes. As they did, Anataalie gave each of the ladies a gown of velvet, splendid couture pieces from Paris. She smiled and said, keep trim, keep fit, that should be worn when your child graduate.

And so the rest of the day was quiet, the rest of the group was taking rest in his or her respective cabin. In fact one couple was left. As they came for supper they were surprised to be alone. Yusuf smiled and said:

"The pull of Louis Armstrong was too strong and that the blues in the three black couples took them away, as they needed to feel the land under the feet to dance."

The white couple laughed and soon forgot all about others, as the dinner was indeed splendid. He asked Peter, the white man: so what are you doing now? Peter replied:

" Well, I do not have many resources, but I like to keep busy, my wife and me are trying to see if we could run our own garage, I am a fine mechanic, you know."

The dinner was a real gourmet treat: it felt almost like a Christmas dinner. Then at about 3 am, Yusuf wished everyone good night and went to his room.

Anataalie was left with the couple and said:

"Well, I must confess that we knew about your garage project, and in fact Yusuf has bought it. "

Peter was shocked.

Anataalie laughed:

"Allow me to explain. Well it is bought in your name, and here is the deed of ownership. You will also receive an initial free investment of 200,000USD. So, I guess you better hurry home and start planning. The couple was speechless, the lady cried. Anataalie laughed again:

"I knew you would cry Marie, so I have bought you a tear drop, an emerald pendant, a small gift from me."

And the couple disembarked in the next few hours.

Then in the evening, Yusuf came down and sat with Anataalie in the dining room. Anataalie asked:

"Yusuf, why?"

Yusuf said gently:

"Anataalie, we know each other for long now. You know how little people care for me and I for them. They had only cared for me because I was wealthy. "

Anataalie bowed her head, yes she knew that well. His wives were fleecing him; his children were ungrateful, his friends always wanting him to fulfil a new request…. He had been deeply hurt in his heart and soul.

Yusuf continued:
" Anataalie, I want you to tell the staff to go home, pay them handsomely, I will take charge of the cruiser on my own. And you too, Anataalie must disembark, I have not forgotten you. You will have all of my wealth."

Anataalie felt a stab in her heart and said nothing. She instructed the staff to disembark. They did.

Yusuf was at last alone. He had done what he thought was best.

He sat on his bed and put a hand on his chest, his heart was in a very very poor condition, the doctor said he had a week left in him at most, the transplant did not work…. He was too tired to go through this again, the hope, the pain, and the dependence on other.

He took a glass of water and put some drops in it, he drank slowly, and he felt the pain leaving him, giving him some space.

He heard a soft noise, the door had opened. Anataalie entered softly.

"Yusuf? Why did you not tell me? "

"Tell you what Anataalie? "Yousuf asked. his voice was very harsh.

"Nothing, Yousuf, nevermind. So what is your plan?" Anataalie continued.

There was a silence what is your plan Yusuf, Anataalie asked again. He was a businessman, she knew he would not evade that kind of question.

She sat besides him. He looked at her; his stare was very hard:
"Well, do you remember Anataalie, when you told me about Jacques Brel the man who sang Ne me quitte pas, If you go away?"

"Yes, I do," Anataalie said. "You liked that tale so much that you named this cruiser after his song."

Then her face froze; her heart felt so cold. She urged:
"Yusuf, please carry on."

But she already knew.

Yusuf said:
" I too, Anataalie, have little time to leave. My heart is not good anymore. And so this is my last trip," his stare grew hard and angry:
"And it is time for you to go, Anataalie, Go, roh (Arabic word for Go away)"

"Yes, later Yousuf". Anataalie said sharply. "Go on Yusuf, tell me more. I deserve to know."

Yusuf went on like a broken record, it was hard for him to explain, and the pain in his chest was excruciating:

"Well, my plan is simple. Over there, in the Faberge diamond encrusted gold egg, there is cyanide. Within an hour I shall take it, and let the boat and the song of Jacques Brel take me to the paradise my soul deserves."

"Yes, Yusuf. I understand. "Anataalie said softly.

She understood that Yusuf had gone into deep pain, his heart was hurting, his face had grown very pale from the pain and he was sweating heavily

" Yes Yusuf, I have understood. But Jacques Brel did not complete the song and so I shall complete it for you."

She went to the Faberge egg, she opened it. She could not stand seeing him in such pain. She quickly brought out two crystal glasses, filled them with water, and dropped half of the quantity in each glass. She took one glass and gave the other one to Yusuf. She said with a smile:
"A votre sante Jacques Brel,"

Yusuf said:
"Ta-aali."

And they drank both to each other, without a word.

In less than a minute, the boat was free, there was no hand alive to guide it, none found it, none looked for it. Taali, the calling in my life.
- The End-

Short Story 14

Hostage, American way

He was looking for a meaning in his life, something that would somehow make his life worthwhile.

He felt empty inside, since his last wife had left him. She had just left without a note or a word, cleaning out his saving account and everything else.

He had nowhere to go and was living with his mother. His mother was a pious person and did not appreciate that he had relented and granted a divorce on mutual grounds to his wife, it was a sin, and so she was going to Church everyday, praying for the salvation of his son's soul.

Indeed, he had looked in his soul to see if a prayer would make the emptiness he felt would go away, but it increased his depressive moods. He went into therapy and Prozac did not seem to help but rather worsen his state.

And so on Sunday, to escape from the oppressive atmosphere of his mother's house and sermons, he would go to the Art Museums, trying to see if he could find any meaning in Art.

He went regularly there, and toured the galleries, but he did not find what he was looking for, the emptiness was so heavy inside of him. He found himself following the tourist groups and the museum guide and absorbing the explanations. They did not seem to make much sense, and the guide was very cold towards him. He was not exactly the museum type; his outfit seemed so out of place.

And so slowly he decided that the Art Museums were not a place for him and started frequenting the sub-art markets, the places where people make things with their hands and sell it to the public. There were lots of Native American arts there, and South American, African.

And soon he found himself returning to one of those tiny markets. There were no guides there and lots of lonely people who were happy to talk to him and for once he felt as if he was above them all. He was seen as a potential buyer. A middle-aged lady who was selling art made of beads fascinated him. Her art did not really appeal to him, but he was amazed at the tiny bundle of money she could make in one afternoon.

The next Sunday he went there and brought his guitar, she let him sit besides him and sing a song, and to his amazement, people started to drop coins in his guitar case. Barbara, the bead lady was happy, she was all smiles. That afternoon he too made a neat bundle of money over a few songs.

They decided to leave the place and go for a cup of coffee at her place. She owned her own house, and that evening he did not go to his mother home to sleep.

The next day, he took Barbara to the Art Museum and repeated to her what the guide had told the tourist, Barbara was so impressed. He told her that he knew that she had that much knowledge too in her heart. He asked her to put her heart against his and look at an artwork, he would know. She was conquered.

That evening, he called his mother to say he won't be in for a week, as he had to fix Barbara's house. His mother cried on the phone, but Barbara was calling him and so he just dropped the phone.

He hardly went back to his mother place any longer, he would help Barbara to fix her house, and there was so much to do, and hours went fast when they went so slowly at his mothers.

And every Sunday, they both went to the market, she sold her beads, he sang away, and both marveled at how easy the tiny bundles of money were made.

Soon he called his mother informing her that he had married Barbara in a civil registry. His mother cried,
Barbara called; he dropped the phone on his mother.

Life was smooth; he was looking towards Sundays.
Barbara has gone obese, she was gluing beads on famous artists posters, calling herself the new Dali and
Her fingers felt so rough when she touched him, but he remembered the neat bundles of money they would both make on Sunday. It was all right.

Soon the business went down, it was harder to get a neat bundle of money at the market since a young lady had set her stall next to Barbara's.

She was a sweet thing of 19 with a porcelain face and big blue eyes, She was doing ladybugs in papier-mâché and she was selling them like hot potatoes. She had a wonderful smile and the customer would buy whatever she would put forward.

And so he left Barbara's stall and went to sit close to the papier-mâché girl, she would blush so easily when he talked to her. He sang a song too at her stall and he made a neat bundle while at her place.

That evening Barbara was mad. She shut the bedroom door on him and told him cruel words.

He felt so cold, he realized that he had not been careful, that all the tiny bundles of money he had given her because she had so many bills to pay for the upkeep of the house. He had nothing.

In the morning she came out of the bedroom he noticed how unattractive she was, how gross, obese and vulgar she looked, she did not say a word.

And so he made her breakfast and explained as to why he had sat with the papier-mâché girl. He explained that it was all for Barbara, as one can only vanquish competition by understanding it. That is what he had been doing.

Barbara smiled, and the door of the bedroom was kept open.

On next Sunday, he helped Barbara install her stall as usual, and then he made a wink at her and went to the papier-mâché girl. She giggled, and blushed as he sang a song he wrote for her. Customers bought everything she had brought, and they also dropped many coins in the guitar's case.

Barbara's stall was desert, she did not even manage to sell one piece.

And before the evening was over, he took the papier-mâché girl outside and did not return to Barbara's for two days. Then he came and smiled shyly telling Barbara: do not worry my darling, everything will be all right. It is done.

Barbara smiled; she had bought him a new shirt too.

That Sunday, they both went to the market, and the stall of the papier-mâché girl was vacant. Barbara sold very well. Many asked about the papier-mâché girl.

One customer bought a few pieces for Barbara, a tourist. He explained that he had hoped to buy papier-mâché art but he was informed that the girl had seemingly committed suicide. So he had to leave and he would require buying 5 items from Barbara. He was in a hurry and did not bargain.

They made a record bundle of money that Sunday and they were both beaming.

Life had taken a routine course, and whenever there were competition, a plan was set up between us so that the neat bundles of money would still be made in good and bad days that was the meaning of the civil marriage of theirs.

Emptiness had crept in his heart again; Barbara would shut the door so often on him on a whim. And he felt so depressed and unloved, he could not say why. And so he sneaked back to his mother and to the Art Museum.

There one day, he met a beautiful young French actress, Anataalie, and she was kind, he told her of the emptiness he felt within him. She smiled softly. He was so taken by her.

She spent hours at the museum, as the Museum had brought in a great Monet collection, and she wanted to feel the French Blue as much as she could, before the collection was taken to another capital of the world.

And so he sneaked often to the Art Museum and he would always find her in the same meditative pause, she was so utterly beautiful, he was smitten.

Barbara had noticed his unexplained absences, and one day she followed him. She saw her and she knew that she was not matching to that woman. She was something else.

But she knew exactly what to do.

And so on that day, Bruce was locked in, he was not allowed out even for a walk. He was to glue the beads on the art posters and clean the house, take care of paper work.

Barbara on the other hand would go out for longer periods; she would stay out overnight. There was nothing he could do; he had no money, no friend.

Strangely enough, the emptiness had left him, his fate was sealed, he had become a kept, a hostage American way. He felt happy in his new condition.

At last he had found his spiritual path, the materialist nirvana of America.

-The End-

SHORT STORY 15

For a handful of Petro Dollars

Kuwait City was vibrant as usual. The luxury cars were cruising the modern high ways, and everyone was lost in their own thoughts. Business meetings, banking, office work. Kuwait was a city a mirage built in the desert. People looked prosperous, and the office building towers were definitely imposing: they could rival easily with any business towers of London or New York.

Yet the difference was felt as soon as one entered any office, and that difference was in the smell of the place: there was the gentle aroma of the Arabian coffee or tea prepared with French cinnamon and mint. The Arabian hospitality was at its best, and the foreign businessman was treated with several of strong Arabian coffee; indeed in the business guide dealing with the Arabian customs, it was mentioned to never to refuse a cup of coffee or tea as this was considered bad manners.

Peter had arrived from London to take up a new position that had been offered to him, at the Kuwait Refinery Company. His contract was a very substantial one, and the salary mentioned there was 10 times what he would earn in any Western city. He had been told that life was harsh, but so far he could not think clearly all: he saw was affluence and abundance everywhere.

The Mandoob (the peon) of the company was at the airport to welcome him. The young man wore a full suit and a tie. And as soon as Peter cleared from the immigration gate, Sayyed greeted him:

"Good morning sir, I hope you had a good journey, my name is Sayyed and I am here to help you."

Sayyed informed Peter that a porter would carry his luggage to the car, not to worry. And they proceeded to the parking area. Sayyed went up to a Grand Motor Limousine Caprice, and opened the door to Peter and told him to sit on the back seat. They were going to the apartment allotted for Peter, as per administrative orders of the Headquarters. It was very hot, inspite of the air-conditioning, Peter was sweating heavily, and pondered at how Sayyed was remaining so unaffected by the heat, how he managed to remain cool, not even sweating. Peter's clothes were soaked with sweat.

The place looked marvelous, it had palm trees and flowers, and luxury cars were everywhere, he had not seen a single smaller car model such as a Ford Escort.

After a while, Sayyed parked besides a luxury building, and addressed him with a proud look on his face:

"Sir, we have arrived."

They took the lift, and Sayyed opened the door to allow Peter enter first. It was a gorgeous place, the apartment was indeed grand, and would suit him and his family when they were ready to arrive, school was still on and his wife Virginia had decided to stay back until the kids had finished the school year. It was a great offer, and they had decided together to go for it.

The floor of the apartment was marbled, there was a huge balcony, and Sayyed handed over to him the keys. Sayyed took leave. The young man said pleasantly:

"The receptionist speaks English, but here is my mobile number do not hesitate to call me any time day or night in case of need. Tomorrow I shall collect you at 12noon to take you to the headquarters."

Peter was happy.

There was a swimming pool on the rooftop and he went to take a swim, it was like a Paradise Island. Then when he felt hungry he rang the receptionist and asked for the meal of the day, the food bill was on the company, he could order anything he wanted to.

The food trolley came very fast, within ten minutes the doorbell rang and the kitchen boy hurried to set the table. Peter ate comfortably, then he called the receptionist to let the kitchen boy come up again and take away the dishes.

"Yes sir"", the receptionist replied, " my name is Abdul-Aziz. Please be advised that the flats get cleaned in the morning and I am personally responsible for the safety of your belongings. Leave your laundry in the laundry bag."

Peter felt happy and called his wife to tell her what a good reception he had been given so far. Virginia , his wife, had been a bit anxious over this new move in Peter's career. Back at home she had heard so many funny stories about the Arabian Gulf. She enquired with anguish over the phone. Peter understood and reassured her and said:

"Really Virginia, it seems to be a nice place. Just wait to see the apartment we have been given."

There was nothing much to do for the day, so he switched on the huge Television set: he could access all the channels of the world, as the TV was connected to a satellite dish.

Oddly late in that evening, there was a ring at his door, he went to open, his neighbor, a gentleman from Iraq, had come to welcome him in the building and he handed over some dates on a tray. The neighbor smiled as he left and said:
"If you need anything let me know.

Peter went to sleep very happy, the bedroom was gorgeous, but then everything was so luxurious: the bathroom was so huge, there were 2 toilets, but the whole flat was so spacious with 3 bedrooms, a reception hall, a dining room, a sitting room and large kitchen.

He set his alarm clock and knew that yes, this country he was going to like a lot.

The next morning, Sayyed rang at his door and enquired whether Peter had faced any problem and whether he was ready to go to the headquarters. Peter was ready they left the residential building.

Sayyed drove some 20mns, away from the city in the desert area, They had reached. In front of them, there was a huge compound in the middle of which an impressive building was standing white and silver.

Sayyed explained to Peter that this was indeed the headquarter, the building had about 10 floors.

The building was very similar to the one Peter had an apartment in, the architecture was the same. Sayyed explained that the apartment building belonged to the company and they had used the same architect. As soon as they stepped in, Peter was taken aback by the buzz of business, everyone looked very busy. The Indian secretaries were typing non-stop on their computers, men in suits kept moving from one office to the next office; some workers with helmets were seated outside the administration office. It had indeed a very busy look.

Sayyed was greeted by everyone, and as he introduced Peter, Peter understood that Sayyed was in fact the private driver of Yusuf, the chairman of the Kuwait Black Oil Company.

Peter was briefly introduced to the Administration Manager, and was ushered hurriedly into the palatial office of Yusuf, or Abu Hamad as he was nicknamed traditionally-father of Hamad, his first born). They said Abu Hamad does not want to wait.

Peter sat down in the leather sofa in the room of the private secretary to the Chairman: A middle aged Palestinian man, Hussein, also in suit, looking very stressed, not daring to look at Peter. He kept his head down and continued working his head down…There was an oppressive feeling all around, and the secretary kept answering calls, he had some six sets. Peter could hear him saying: "Hailer. "(An Arabic word that meant, yes with respect to you), Abu Hamad, yes, " in a very subdued voice. "Peter noticed that everytime the red phone rang, the secretary's face became stressed and panicky, his hands trembled.

Meanwhile Sayyed had opened the heavy rosewood door of the chairman's office, he went inside, and no sound could be heard. Then Sayyed came out, his face pale and stressed. He told Peter:

"Please sir wait, our chairman shall receive you in a minute. Here is Hassan his private secretary, he will take you in the room and when your meeting is over, you can come downstairs in the Administration office so that we set you up in your office."

The silence interrupted by the phone calls was oppressive, an office boy was coming and going with a tray on which stood a crystal glass full of water, waiting outside, again knocking stressed at the door and returning to Hassan's room with the empty glass…

Then the ring came and Hassan said to Peter:
"Yes sir, please do come in."

Peter was introduced into the office of the Chairman.

It was impressive; the walls were paneled with expensive wood, decorated with antiques. But Peter found it so shocking to see that there was nothing on the desk, not a paper, not a magazine, absolutely nothing, not even a pen, a bare and very expensive desk. Then he noticed a huge leather chair in which a man in the traditional dress of the country the long pure white dishdasha and the white cloth set with a black rope around the skull was seated. He was still mystified by the bare desk, only later would he understand that the true sign of wealth was the absence of a need to do anything at all. And this that was one of the many symbolims of prestige of the very wealthy of those countries.

He looked at Abu Hamad and was unsure how to start, but as he focused on the face of the man, he saw a face heavily marked by stress and a very sharp pair of eyes, not unkind, the pair of eyes of a business tycoon. He could relate to that man, yes he felt it in his guts, he could indeed relate to Yusuf.

Abu Hamad said in very good English:
"So Peter, welcome to the company. How was your journey? "
At this point the trembling office boy came in and served coffee to Yusuf and Peter. Yusuf said:
"Drink my friend."

Peter could relate to that man. As they drank coffee, Yusuf asked:

"How was your journey? "
Peter replied:
"Thank you, the flat is lovely. "

Yusuf turned his face away and Peter understood that this should not be discussed here.

Yusuf asked him about his hometown in England. He seemed to enjoy Peter 's conversation, ten minutes had elapsed and Yusuf reached for a button under his desk, it was a ring for the secretary to come in. Immediately, Hassan came in with an anxious look on his face and without looking at Yousuf told Peter:

"Yes, Sir let me show you your office."

Peter understood that the meeting was over. Yusuf did not move, and Peter made an awkward exit, Yusuf has ceased to acknowledge his existence and was looking through the window. Peter hesitantly and unsure just said:

"Thank you, I am pleased to be working for your company."

Yusuf did not respond or shifted his gaze from his window.

Hassan closed the door behind as they exited with utmost care, not to make a sound, so it appeared to Peter.

As soon as he exited this area, everything seemed so relaxed. And he settled down in his job, his office was good. Everything that was promised in the contract he had signed back in England was granted to him.

He loved his job. Though he had to go to the oil refinery plants everyday. And the heat was hard to bear at first it was so hot, very hot, but he had been given a great car, brand new, and the air-conditioning system was strong. His office at the plant was also fully air-conditioned.

His family has recently come to join him, the kids were going to the New English school, the company driver were in charge of driving them there and bringing them back

Life was luxurious, entertaining, and the money was great.
They had made a very good decision.

A year had elapsed, Peter did not get to meet Yusuf again, he was never called in his office, and none wanted to speak about him. Yusuf was a multi-millionaire; his staff loved him but feared him at the same time. Nothing was known about him except that he had several houses all over the world. Peter did not question; somehow he understood that questions were not welcomed when it came to Yusuf. Yet he could remember the sharp and intelligent look in Yousuf's face, the sophistication in the way he spoke to him.

None knew when Yusuf would be in the office, or whether he would come at all, none would raise a word.

366 days had passed. One morning, the Administration Manager came in his office and said:
"Hi Peter, how are things with you today?"

Peter smiled he liked the guy, he was a good man, an Egyptian, he saw how he treated the field workers and the office staff, he was a fair man, a kind man. He said:

"Good morning Abdul-Rahim, how are things with you, have a seat, take a coffee with me."

Peter had learnt fast how to deal with people of this region. Abdul Rahim sat and said:

"Well Peter, I have a very good news, Yusuf called me and instructed me to raise your rank from chief-engineer of the plant to the rank of General Manager and your salary is doubled."

Peter was shocked.

How would that be? After all, he did never meet with Yusuf after that first meeting. But he did not ask questions.
Abdul Rahim continued:

"Well tomorrow morning, I will come to the field and meet you at your field office, and I shall bring the new contract with me for your signature. The terms are the same, except that your rank has been upgraded and your income doubled."

Peter was very pleased. He called his wife and told her the news: he said we should go to the Sheraton Hotel tonight and have a party. They had a lovely time by the pool, a barbecue party.

Next morning Peter drove to the field, and went on with his work. It was a hard work, and they were testing the new pumps for the oil refinery plants.

At about 11am, a car that he had never seen before came in the area, the guard did not check the id of the driver as he usually did, and immediately opened the gate.

The car coming in was a Mercedes of golden color. The windows were dark, and Peter could not see the face of this visitor. Was it an inspector from the Ministry? He was not sure but everyone came out, and stood outside. He was bewildered.

Then the Mercedes stopped in front of Peter's office and Abdul-Rahim came out, ran to the backside and opened the door; Yusuf stepped out of the car.

In the daylight, Yousuf's clothing was so very white, whiter than any white clothes he had ever seen. He saw the dazzle of the diamond dial of the Rolex watch on Yusuf wrist, and the traditional Tasbih (traditional beads string) in his hand, that were dazzling too, they were precious stones. Yousuf looked younger and taller than Peter remembered him.

Everyone stood outside and bowed their heads, their chins on their chests. None moved or said a word.

Abdul Rahim hurried ahead and opened Peter's office door and addressed Yusuf:

"Please Abu Hamad come in."

At once Peter rose, and Abdul Rahim proceeded to clean the chair in front of Peter, and Yusuf sat silently.

Abdul Rahim addressed Peter:

"Here is your contract, please sign."

Peter did not dare to read the contract, the gaze of Yusuf was hypnotic, and the emanation coming from that man was of strong inner strength and a will of steel.

Peter signed the papers and looked again in Yusuf 's eyes, for the second time since his arrival in this country. Once again, he felt himself impressed by the muted intellectual sharpness in the Tycoon's eyes. Peter just uttered:

"Thank you, Sir."

Yusuf did not reply.

Abdul Rahim felt contented as he took the contract papers away, things were fine.

Then Yusuf said in his sophisticated English:

"Since I am here Peter, I might as well see the new pump we purchased."

Peter was surprised: How and why the tycoon knew of this tiny insignificant purchase, a few thousand dinars that he had recommended. His mind raced. But Yusuf had already stood up, Abdul Rahim was signaling him to hurry, and so Peter went to show the new piece of machinery.

Yusuf was shown the new purchase.

Yusuf said:

"Well yes, I see it. But how does it work? Show me."

Everyone was still standing outside motionless, heads bowed, and inspite of the intense heat. None had moved.

Peter said:
"Yes, I will show you, of course."

He proceeded to show the mechanism of that engine and switched it on. But then something happened that Peter would never forget in his life.
The engine ejected a flow of oil and one tiny drop went on the white robe of Yusuf.

All of a sudden, the day turned into a nightmare.
It was an insult;

It was something that was not done. Yusuf's face had become very hard and cruel.

Peter felt himself being seized by a group of workers and Yusuf retreated to his Mercedes with Abdul Rahim. Abdul Rahim spat on

Peter and tore the contract he just signed. Peter's mind went wild; it was but a tiny so tiny spot. Why were they behaving this way?

The Mercedes drove away, and Peter felt blow after blow and he was left badly beaten up in the sand. He laid unconscious for a few hours, on regular interval, he felt people passing by, spitting on him.

The evening had come. Sayyed had been sent to pick him up, his wife and children were in the car, very pale. Sayyed pulled Peter from the sand and pushed him in the back seat of the car, like a dirty laundry bag.

Sayyed said harshly to Virginia:
"Clean up your husband, do not say a word, I will help you, and I am taking you all to the airport, just leave."

Peter heard the hostess in the plane to London asking:
"Sir, are you all right."

He said:
"Yes Miss thank you. I had a bit of an accident. Nothing much, I will be all right."

In the microphone, the voice of the captain was heard:

"In a few hours we shall reach Heathrow airport, the weather is cool, and we expect no delay."

-The End-

SHORT STORY 16

The Footsteps in his words

It was a tiny place, yet it felt immense like a quiet sea of greenery…The wind was playing the grass blades like a violin, the music immediately reached my soul as I came closer and closer to the huge white colonial house, which had a desolate look about it now…. None was living there any longer….

I came closer to the wind and stayed lifeless for a few seconds…Yes, I recognized the tune, it played the tune of the last ball at the Governor's place years ago…For a moment, I could see there in the ballroom the proud English ladies seated with pretty porcelain cups of tea in their hands…they looked so ravishing…Yet, I felt uneasy and as I looked towards the buffet, there in the darkness, I felt the bright stare of the Indian boy dressed in a silly uniform and his eyes spoke of hatred and humiliation , and suddenly I heard the cup falling from the white gloved hand of the proud lady…….It made a soft noise on the parquet floor….

The governor gave a hard look to the lady, his wife, the hostess…And she in turn gave him back a hard look and suddenly the ballroom had become a mirror gallery where stares of hatred were thrown from wall to wall…And I felt unwanted, I felt like crying…but I could not shed a tear…I did not even know why?

And I looked away at the window, and I left the governor's place orchestra music for the music that the wind was playing with the blades of the grass…Once one English man had been calling my name, he said I was the footsteps in his words, always would be so

My feet were hurting…. I had walked such a long distance…. The footsteps in his words…. I came for those…they were not here again this summer, none had come…none called me anymore I did not recognize anyone, and yet everyone saluted me and said "mamma, can we give you a lift"…In the eyes of the poor man, there was no hatred for me…Why. Did not I wear white gloves too like the English ladies…?

And I looked at my hands, as if I woke from a sad dream, my hands were of copper color with gold rings on my finger…. My dress was of incredible beauty, sky blue and gold…. And my hair long and scented with flowers…I could feel the gentle weight of my long silky terse in my back reaching down to my waist…

And all of a sudden, I understood that I was not from the Governor's house, why did I think of going there, I belonged to the Maharaja's house…. I was one of his daughters…. The footsteps in his words…. Like a mantra, my heart was void…. And so painful since then. Why did he have to leave for London? His majesty's orders he explained, I must…

Yes why do I keep coming here, none called me anymore so beautifully: the footsteps in his words. My love, why have you not come again as you promised? My heart aches so much….

The white Benz was waiting for me, the driver begged me good evening and said: mamma, please come in the car as he held the door of the car open.

I lifted my silk skirt and was dazzled and anguished by the diamond anklet of my right ankle, the magic was magnetic.... A white strong hand held my ankle for a split of a second as I stepped in the limousine, and the electricity going through my body then brought me back memory of who I truly was, I was the mistress the one who wants and the one who gets all that she wants.... all but the call of the footsteps in his words...all but this calling in my life

I entered the car, and sat in the plush red velvet back seat...he was there, his blue eyes looked in mine as I locked the stare into mine until I mastered his resolve....He remained motionless and repeated the same ritual as always...he poured some drinks, pulled the curtain over the window separating the driver seat from the back compartment, he added some ice in the drink and brought it to my lips as he removed the hair pin and freed the nappe of my hair...I was of royal blood, and I kept my stare on him as he took some ice cubes and pushed them in the front of my silk blouse. I pushed him back with my right feet, and sharply ordered him to make himself ready.

He was an hypnotized pray, he surrendered his pride and became the toy of the spoilt little girl, one garnment at a time, he peeled, nothing moved in my face, my mind was following the journey of the melting of the cold liquidified ice cubes to my naked navel, meeting one more sparking diamond, the gold chain around my waist reminded me of the chains of passion I once shared with the calling in my life: the footsteps in his words . My lonely love....my heart was aching as the man next to me suffered the agony of the mere lust of the earth, when I agonized over the eternity void in my heartbeat.

His breathing was so heavy, I let him there in pure humiliation in front of me....I looked at him without moving, until he cried out for me, and when he finally dared to catch my ankle in desperation to bring me down to him, cruel, so cruel I scarred his pale face with a swift movement of my ankle, the diamond of the anklet cut his left cheek, a deep cut and blood started pouring from the fresh wound. I watched in gentle fascination. Now yes now I was ready to receive him.

From Mamba to Bavnaghar, the diamond sparkled in the shade of the ruby love.... Silent and fiery.... For several hours.

Then the palace of my family was to be seen ahead, I retied the strings of my clothing, redid my tress, and told him out without a word. He begged me for another time, and I said not now, goes...and I watched him receding to the size of a red ant in the distance. Like others before him, I would become but another point in time, a useless clue...

He would never see me again, he was marked by the payel diamond, he was done, scared no good anymore...I would need a new one, a fresh face to scar...so easy to find, so easy to use, so easy to forget.

Father was not at home, only the servants...I went to the servants quarter, the girls were singing and dancing.... I watched over and joined in the Danchi became bored soon and, I clapped my finger and chose one servant whose face has been mutilated many times over, his eyes were fiery.... He would stay the night with me, there was no need of diamond trails on his face any more, and he had been tamed...many nights over, a native toy...

Now time was short, tomorrow father will come home and we always are very busy at this time of the year. Yes tomorrow we would fly to

London… and like every year since the last five years I would search for him everywhere in London, I would listen to all the calls to find the calling of my life, I would listen in so intently everywhere I went, I would walk in the rain, go to the theatre, dance in the clubs, go to libraries, play tennis, be in all the places he talked to me about then, in the hope to find him just for a short while again and hear his voice calling me just once more time: come to me you the footsteps in my words..

The calling in my life
Were my footsteps in his words?
Would I find you there, my darling?
I would be good, I promise.

-The End-

Short Story 17

Shall I see you tomorrow?

thoughts, but then she understood that she had started to dislike Suaad, she could not help but see in her mind the red and humiliated faces of the musicians as they were ousted from the Anataalie had just come back from her trip to Egypt. It was a normal business trip, in fact she had been sent by a royal family of the Arabian Gulf to contact Suaad, a famous Egyptian lady singer, who was the most talented in singing the hit songs of the late Empress of all songstresses: Oum Khoulthoum. Oum had been the most famous singer of Egypt, now that she had passed away, her songs were even more in demand. Suaad was indeed the voice that could best render the soulful melodies of the late Oum Khoulthoum.

Anataalie had met Suaad briefly in Egypt. Suaad was indeed very busy shuttling between recording studios. She had signed on many contracts for CDs and tapes, and film scenes, and her schedule was very tight.

Suaad was a petite woman of 40 years old, plump with a cheerful face. She was not beautiful, just attractive, comely. She smiled a lot and she welcomed Anataalie warmly.

The terms of the contract were discussed: she was to sing at one reception held in London in the Hilton Hotel for one night. It was a private reception in honor of the graduation from Oxford of the son of one Arabian King. The son had always been fond of Oum Khoulthoum's songs and had all her CDs. He knew all of her songs by heart, and from the heart.

Oum Khoulthoum had sung the most profound poems of love and arabism with great passion and depth. Arab land. Oum Khoulthoum had become a legend, and her status not only equaled Elvis Presley of America, but also surpassed it many times over. After all, you could easily go for many months without hearing Elvis. In the Arab world, you could not spend a day without hearing the legendary voice.

The deal was made, and Suaad was paid a few thousand dollars as advance and she would be flown in a private jet, and housed at the Hilton too. Her husband was to accompany her and all his expenses would be paid as well.

The Egyptian arrived at Heathrow Airport on schedule and Anataalie had been sent to receive them. Suaad looked in the foggy airport the same as she had back in Egypt, sweet and plain. Mohammed her husband was a tall youngish man of 45, slim and a bit bald. But energy seemed to flow from him, and he was very protective of his wife.

Suaad had been married four times already and had nine children. Mohammed was her latest husband. He was an engineer by profession, but had given his work to be with his wife, he had traveled the world many times over as she was in great demand.

Soon they reached the hotel, and everything was set. There was not time to lose. The morning was booked for the rehearsal of Suaad. The stage props, the sound system had been tested.

Suaad arrived, wearing an expensive dress and was fully made up. The musician had taken place on the stage, and the rehearsal began. When the melody started, Anataalie closed her eyes, listening to Suaad's suave voice. The words were exquisite, of a deep beauty. She sounded so much like the late Oum Khoulthoum.

All of a sudden, the song had stopped: Suaad was standing angry over at one of the violin player, she was actually stomping and screaming with rage...Mohammed, her husband, had gone quickly up to his wife and was talking her down. She was having a fit of rage, and a rictus of anger had ploughed her smooth skin from the nose to the corner of her mouth. Anataalie was shocked. Mohammed had brought his wife a glass of juice and the make-up lady was re-touching Suaad's make-up, while the violin player left the stage, crushed with shame.

The rehearsal started again, and the same incident happened again and again. The musicians in the orchestra had dwindled from 27 to 19. The atmosphere was tense, and so Anataalie decided to leave and stay by the swimming pool, away from the tension.

As soon as she left the room, she could hear the songs sang perfectly one after the other. She enjoyed them from afar. There were no more interruptions, fits of rage.

Strangely, it seemed that somehow her leaving the rehearsal room had soothed Suaad's mood. Anataalie smiled why was she thinking illogical rehearsal.

Meanwhile Mohammed came out towards the swimming pool as his wife continued rehearsing. He was pale and distraught.

He said in a polite tone:
"Please Mademoiselle, forgive my wife, she is always a bit edgy before performances.

Anataalie smiled back:
"It is fine, Mohammed, I do understand."

Mohammed replied"
"No, Anataalie, you do not understand."

Anataalie was puzzled:
"Why are you saying this? What is it that I do not understand?"

Mohammed looked intently in Anataalie's eyes.
" Suaad is no fool. She already knows."

"She knows what? I do not follow you," replied Anataalie.

In the distance Anataalie saw the general manager of Hilton coming towards them. Anataalie rose and told Mohammed:
"Please, let me introduce you to Ghassan, the general manager of the hotel. "
Ghassan was a charming Palestinian man and he was happy to meet Mohammed. Soon both of them left the area to go to the coffee shop.

Anataalie felt so exhausted, she relaxed in the chair all alone in the swimming pool area and closed her eyes. She fell asleep.

Suddenly she felt herself being pushed brutally her into the swimming pool. She was shocked, but she was a good swimmer, she came back to the surface. She looked around, none was there, and she hurried to her room without anyone seeing her. What had happened there? She did not understand, but she decided that she would keep this incident silent. After all this party was very important, and her present employer would probably not appreciate if she would bring up her personal problems to them on a day like this.

She changed her clothing for a new dry set and came down to the rehearsal hall; Suaad was singing her heart away. She had the symbolic handkerchief a la Oum Khouthoum in her right hand. Oum Koulthoum used to keep one handkerchief in her right hand while singing her songs that were hours long

Suaad's voice was magical, she was immensely talented and she sang song after song.

Anataalie's heartbeat went faster when Suaad started a song that was the favorite of Anataalie: Will I see you tomorrow? Her heart dissolved over and over with every new intonation in Suaad's voice.

As the rehearsal ended, Mohammed came in the rehearsal hall, helping his wife come down the stage, bringing her drink, talking to her, laughing. Anataalie went over to Suaad and said:

"Madame Suaad, you sing so beautifully, you have indeed enchanted me"

Suaad smiled, quickly replying:

"Thank you, thank you, thank you. Come and eat with us."

Anataalie smiled and thanked Suaad. They all went to the Private Dinning Room and were served traditional Arabian dishes: kebabs, and meshawis, tabouleh, dozens a dishes.

It was a musician party; Suaad was the guest of honor and every musician felt honored to be there, sitting by her side. Mohammed whispered to his wife:
"Eat well my darling. I must go to see Ghassan to see that all goes well for you tonight".

He was to see the general manager to discuss some acoustic problem; Suaad had been displeased about it.

It was a nice party, a friendly party, Suaad joked a lot, and her face was so attractive when she laughed, her teeth were dazzling, her cheeks slightly flushed. She made Anataalie laugh too

The lunch was over and everyone went to his or her room for a rest to be ready for tonight event. Everyone was very excited about it. The anticipation was great, the patron was a very wealthy man, if the songs pleased him, he could shower on impulses, thousands of dollars on the stage, on the performer.
Anataalie took the lift to retire to her private room and prepare herself for the party.

She went to the closet where the maid had previously hanged all her precious haute couture gowns; she had not yet made her mind which garments she would wear. As she opened, a small cry escape from her lips: All of her gowns had been torn to pieces. They were rags, unrepairable. She was perplexed: who would do such a thing?

As she stood there in shock, there was a knock at thee door. It was Suaad's husband, Mohammed. He said

"I wanted to drop by come and say hello."

Anataalie was almost crying, from the shock of seeing her garments ruined. She said:
"It is not a very good time Mohammed, besides I do not like to invite people into my hotel room. You should know that it would not be polite for me to invite you in."

Mohammed laughed:
"Do you call that immense suite, a hotel room, surely not?"

Anataalie said:
"Alright, come in, but just for a moment. I take it you have something important to discuss."

Mohammed had an honest face. As he sat, the room service had brought some tea. Mohammed asked:
"What is it Anataalie, you seem out of sort?"

She said curtly: "
"Yes, I am a little bit disturbed but it nothing that may concern you Mohammed, it is just that someone has ravaged my dresses."

He became puzzled and asked:
"What do you mean? "

She stood up and opened her closet, she said:
"Well, look for yourself."

He was shocked.

"Yes, it is a very mean thing to do,"

Anataalie said:
"Anyway, whoever did this, was not successful entirely because you see the dress I am going to wear tonight will arrive from my the tailor today, I had sent it for some minor adjustments two hours ago."

She kept quiet on the Swimming Pool incident.

Mohammed said softly:
"Anataalie, I am so sorry really. And I must apologize to you, you see I came here to tell you that I am in love with you Anataalie"

Anataalie laughed:
Ahh, Mohammed, what a joker you make. Please stop this, this is all too absurd. Are you playing a game?"

Mohammed looked grave:
"Why do you laugh Anataalie, I meant what I said: I do love you."

Anataalie stood up and said coldly:
"You must leave Mohammed, this can never be between us. You know that. Please leave."

Mohammed was pale and stressed; the rejection had hit him hard in the heart.

The evening came at last. Suaad was splendid in her long peach velour gown.

Soon the royal family came and they sat by the stage, they were about a hundred people, and Misha'al the young man who graduated from Oxford was the closest to the stage.

Suaad sang song after song; everyone was enthralled by her performance. Anataalie felt the gaze of Mohammed on her, but did not react. She behaved as if she did not notice. He left, pale and distraught.

Then the young Arabian prince went on the stage and said a word to Suaad while showering her with thousand of Dollars. He wanted Suaad to sing
Will I see you tomorrow?
The favorite of Anataalie.
Suaad started the song, and everyone was mesmerized by the charisma she sent to the audience with each and every word. Anataalie felt every word as if some unknown hand was carving them in her heart.

At break time, Suaad rested in her changing room and Anataalie went to see her.

Suaad was mad with anger and screamed at her:
"Oh yes, you the shameless lying French b..ch". I know your king, have no dignity, and go away. Why did you entice my husband? Go away I hate you. You are not the first one you know and will not be the last. But I am here and I watch over him to guard him against money diggers like your kind."

Anataalie was shocked. She did not want to upset the Diva; but she thought best not to offer any explanation and to just leave. Just a few hours to go. She could manage this, at the very least. She certainly did not want to spoil the soiree of Misha'al.

As she went away, Mohammed was standing anxious, outside the changing room in the darkness:
"Anataalie, may I ask you to reconsider."

Anataalie replied:
"No Mohammed my answer is final. Please do not bring this absurd subject between us ever again."

She waited and thought for a while. She asked Mohammed:
" Mohammed, before you leave, would you tell me that much: is it you that tore up my dresses and pushed me in the swimming pool.

Mohammed replied:
" No, Anataalie, of course it cannot be me, what are you thinking? It was not I. It was Suaad, she gets insanely jealous. She does those things."

Anataalie sighed:
"Anyway by tomorrow every one of us will go different ways, and it is for the best I think."

Suaad had got back on stage and sang the song that the young prince has asked her to perform, once more…Will I see you tomorrow…

Many cried, and the young prince was ecstatic. Before Suaad ended the song, the royal cousin went to the stage, he was the second in line to the throne, and he went to Suaad, showered her with more thousand dollars and asked to sing again the song for the third time.

Suaad sang again the same tune, yet in the ending, there was a change, a turn of phrase, she sang: "
la,la,la
No, no and no (in English).

An uneasy silence clouded for a while the party, they resented the change in the ending. But Suaad had already started singing the next song, and everything went back to normal.

The party had been a success. Anataalie returned to her room, and she received a tray with dates and Arabian coffee. She smiled. The room service boy explained:
"This is a gift from the royal family. "

As she drank the coffee, she felt numbness all over the body. She trembled for a while and her heart stopped beating. Life had gone from her.

In the royal suite of the kind, Ghassan asked me:
"Your Excellency, with all due respect, why did this had to be done here? It is going to be difficult to handle with the local authorities".

The old man said:
"This had to be done, for the sake of my beloved country. Misha'al had fallen badly for this woman, that party was for her. He was asking her indirectly for a date. We could never approve a liaison of that sort, and you know that. Anataalie was a very beautiful and intelligent woman, but she was not from royal lineage, neither was she Arab. Just manage it anyway you can, your expenses will be covered.

A shot gun sound was heard throughout the floor, the young prince, t came out, flood was gushing out from the gunshot wound on his left temple, he collapsed on the floor and his last words were:

"Anataalie
Will I see you tomorrow?
Where you have gone, I am going
Do wait for me.
Ta-aa-li, the calling in my life."

-The End-

SHORT STORY 18

The Secret of the Stone

The church bells were ringing for Sunday mass in the spring day of this wonderful April in a small village of Greece. The way to the church was lined with trees of jasmine and blue bells and the soft breeze was delicately scented with the flower fragrances.

The fumet of the Sunday meals prepared in the kitchen by the women, came by intermittent clouds, the lamb roast was in the oven and would be ready to be taken to the dinner table when everyone would be back after mass.

Everyone, or almost except for a few view, was making their way to the old church, attired in their best clothes, and smelling of French Eau de Cologne.

One mother, a widow, was glowing with pride in seeing all her daughters walking besides her, all four in the same dress pattern she had labored over, for months, with love, to make ready for this day . A pink organza skirt with a violet purple bodice. Everyone was looking at the four young girls who already looked strikingly beautiful with their olive skin, heavy dark locks, and slender bodies. They would become beauties in a year or two and the matrons were eyeing them carefully to see if they could be a suitable match for their sons.

The mass went as usual, nothing much to say the priest had dispensed his Sunday benediction and all the souls were in harmony with the seasons of the earth until next Sunday.

Entire families walked down slowly to their village happy, the children running and giggling ahead, trying to catch butterflies, young girls whispering to each other and blushing…The mother looked on and smiled, they discussed the price of food and schooling. Behind were the young men, the bachelors, smoking and standing tall…they would make something of themselves they told each other so. They had known each other since birth. In this village there had been till now but one clinic and one school, one church, on rail station, one butcher shop…. Everyone knew each other. But things were changing, they saw it happen, and it was thrilling to their young minds.

It was another spring Greek Sunday, and so, tables had been pulled outside and each family took place around the table, and the matrons brought out the Sunday meal. The traditional dishes of lamb roast, Greek salads and the mousaka were put in large tray on the grand table. The elder cut the lamb and everyone went ahead and ate heartily, after all they had no worries left, and the Church took care of healing their wounds.

The meal was over and everyone took their usual place in the lush grass in front of their houses: girls were singing schools songs, the little ones had fallen asleep in the lap of their mothers and the older men were sipping some liquor watching the younger ones play the Petanque.

Everyone was there, except for Pierre, who lived in a very poor habitat on the outskirts of the village. Closer to the cliffs and the sea. Pierre had been the only non-Greek for a while, and he was well accepted by the village, as he was a trouble-less and a gentle soul. Pierre was from French Brittany, a young man with pale blue eyes and blond wavy hair. He had come to Greece a few years ago and had stayed on. He would spend his free time painting Nature mortes, scenarios, And he was seen often, seated in the sand, making sketches on rough papers, for hours on end. He did not talk much and shied away from the villagers. But they knew him as a good and decent man, someone not afraid to help when it was needed…He was a good mecanician and would not hesitate to repair a scooter or a car. Often too, the villagers would call on him to help them understand some French tourists who did not know Greek or English. He would come any time of day or night: he would take no money, no matter how much they insisted. They respected him.

He was known also to be employed on a part time basis as a caretaker of the grand villa of a French Actress. .

Anataalie had arrived to the village a year ago and had bought a secluded villa to escape the paparazzi.

Of course, the entire village had prospered because of her presence. Since it became known to the world that she lived in the remote village, tourists had started to come to this place, and the dollars started to flood in: the tourist business boomed, and in summer and spring, many were taking lodging with the villagers, in the hope that they could steal a glimpse of her. Her coming had indeed been a blessing to that otherwise forsaken and impoverished village

She was very reclusive and the villagers hardly saw her at all, she did not even go to the golden beach that was walled and had been made as part of her territory to enable her enjoy the sea without being bothered by unwanted voyeurs.

They did not know much about Anataalie the actress, as she was called. All they knew came from the daughter of a villager, Alia, who was employed too in the household.

Alia had narrated that Anataalie liked to be alone and did not speak much, but when she did she spoke with a soft voice. The villager daughter always added when asked about it, that it did not matter to her much that Anataalie was so silent. When they questioned her about the silence, Alia quickly replied that if one saw her beautiful face, one would know that she was like an angel, there was a light of serenity about her. And that she was simple…and so very sad too.

The villager daughter said she did not know what to say more about Mademoiselle Anataalie because that is all she had seen really. But she loved that woman, she said with tears in her eyes, she was such a beautiful and fragile person. She said that Anataalie cried when tourists wanted to come near her, she became frightened and got with each new intrusion wounded in the heart

And so Alia told all the villagers to try and help the lonely actress, and reminded them, that it was Anataalie that had brought a new prosperity to the village, and that none should sell the privacy of the actress. They all agreed and it was the village's secret pact.

Pierre had been hired as the caretaker, and he was called upon some-times to take care of the plumbing, or for cleaning the swimming pool of the actress's place.

Life had turned for the best now in the village: every young man and girl were now assured a job, the future was not bleak any longer…They were proud of the constructions that were going on, new hotels, with tennis courts…Old Greek cafes were now expanding and their façades had been redone and they were now looking like exclusive restaurants of Athena, life was good, and on this day of spring, everyone felt lucky.

It was indeed a wonderful Sunday, and when the villagers heard that Anataalie had arrived in the villa the previous night, they knew that within a few hours dozens of tourists would flood in the village. It would be hard work but it was a new lease on life for the village and everyone was ready to work hard.

Meanwhile, the villa of the actress had become alive though every-thing felt silent and serene. The interior décor was intriguely Spartan, as Anataalie had always refused to furnish it. The whole villa was airy, yet the walls of the villas were covered in books. There was no picture…. There was just a partition where she kept closets for her clothes, which she rarely unpacked and kept in her luggage, to the dismay of the vil-lager's daughter. There was no bed except for a carpet and it was assumed she slept there, on the floor. Only the kitchen had a table and a few chairs. Nonetheless, it was a magnificent place and its only orna-ments seemed to be the sunrays playing on the walls.

Those came through the French window bare glass doors that gave way to Anataalie's private sea beach, and she went there only at night in a retreated corner where no tourist would ever see her even if they did managed to climb up the wall…. She had two huge German shepherd dogs that protected the boundaries of her territory.

Tonight, she was wearing a long white robe, and she had let her hair loose, she looked ravishing in the moonlight. She walked barefoot on the sand beach, a sad and deeply gentle smile on her face. She loved to be that alone, it made her feel secure…The dogs were away, they knew that their mistress did not like to be flanked, they understood it in their beast' hearts. Anataalie valued animals' intelligence, and she was very fond of the sea. She secretly met Jean Cousteau, and was known to have boarded the Calypso often for long trips on the seas of the world.

Suddenly, there was a growl coming from the dogs, Natalie said aloud: "What is it?"
As she followed the dogs, she saw a shadow climbing over the walls, jumping over and landing on the sand beach: the growls ceased…It was Pierre.

Anataalie relaxed and smiled as she walked towards him. They soon were close to each other.
Pierre said:
"Anataalie, I saw you coming and I came to wish you a safe stay"

Anataalie smiled:
"Yes, Pierre, that is so very nice of you. Thank you. Let us sit and talk for a while"

They sat apart from each other and watched the gentle waves of the Night Sea. She asked:
"How have you been doing, Pierre?"

Pierre looked into Anataalie's eyes:
"Fine, anataalie, fine."

She continued:
"Pierre, I saw your mother while I was in France, she is well.

Pierre kept silent.

Anataalie continued:
"Pierre, I came to know that your mother is sending you half of her widow pension. It must be hard for her to live on such a small income, and it must be hard for you too, so little money to live on.

Pierre said dryly:
"She is my mother, she decides what she wants to do with her money, what is it to you?"

Natalie closed her eyes:
" Pierre, why is it that you will not take my money. I have so much, I really do not care for it, please accept it from me."

He curtly said:
"Natalie, we have discussed this already, I said no, please let us not discuss this subject again."

She said:
"Why? I do not understand you at all"

He said angrily:
"Why what, Anataalie? It is none of your business."

She did not react to his rudeness; it was the way that he was. He was so terribly poor, it hurt her to see how thin and pale he was, the tiredness in his eyes, his coarse clothing. She wanted him to be well, why did he not accept anything from her? But she knew that if she spoke one more word on this he would leave and perhaps never come back.

She said:
"Yes Pierre all right."

Then she noticed that he had brought with him a bag, it looked a bit heavy.
"What have you brought Pierre?"

He smiled, and to see him smile made her heart rejoice. He smiled so rarely. He looked so handsome, when he did though.
He said:
"Well, you know that before being a painter, I am foremost a sculptor and I have been working on one sculpture since the last three years."
She teased him:
"Yes I know. You spend all of your nights working over that sculpture, I heard about it, but none saw it yet."

Pierre smiled again:
"Anataalie, I have finished it and I am very happy with it. I think it is my best piece and I brought it here tonight to show you."

He paused and remained silent for a while.

She became intrigued:
"Can you show it to me, Pierre? I would really like to see it."

Pierre said:
"Yes, but you and I will be the only one you will get to see for a long time."

She did not understand his meaning. But it did not matter, he sometimes talked in enigmas, she was used to it by now.

She just followed his movements, and he slowly brought out a bust sculpted in Greek soft pale blue marble. When he took it completely out and the bag had fallen empty in the sand; he raised it in the light of the moon and laughed:
"Yes, it is my best piece, come Anataalie look."

Anataalie gasped:
"It was her! He had sculpted her face in the pale blue marble and it was so incredibly remarkable. She raised her hand and touched the forehead of the bust; it felt warm and soft. It was of an incredible workmanship; every line of her features had been engraved so carefully…she did not know what to say…

Then, Pierre placed the bust carefully in the sand, and said
"Anataalie, I have come here with a mission"

She did not understand what he meant, but once again did not question, he did not like questions.

He asked:
"Anataalie, might we go on your yacht now?
She agreed, taken by surprise: it was the first time he had asked her for something.

They walked to the yacht away from each other and boarded it. She boarded the boat by herself, he knew she would not accept his help, his hand. He had taken the bag and the bust with him, and started the Hyatt's engine and went further into the sea …The sea was eerily beautiful tonight, and Anataalie felt the beauty of it all and surprised herself to feel so happy She was not sure why but suddenly everything felt so very bright like a new season, a new spring.

After a while, Pierre stopped the engine, took a clip from his pocket and pinched his nostrils with it. Anataalie looked at what Pierre was doing, not even wondering what he was going to do. She did not really care, the night was beautiful.

She felt hypnotized as she saw him, going overboard with the bag, and he was diving deep. Soon he had reached the bed of the sea.

He looked for a safe place and removed the bust from the bag and placed the sculpture he had been working night after night for the last three years there. It was so uniquely beautiful on the seabed.

His ears started ringing and his eyes were burring, his lungs were in need for oxygen and he came back to the surface.

He climbed up the yacht and Anataalie asked:
"Pierre, am I safe now?"

" Yes Anataalie, you are safe now"

He started the yacht again and they reached back to the beach. Pierre berthed the yacht, and she saw him in his wet clothes climbing back over the boundary walls, without a word

The night was full, the time was full. The spring will be marvelous....

She lied down on the beach and slept there peacefully for the first time in years.

-The End-

Short Story 19

The Green Bird

It was pitch dark in the remote village in Palestine.

In one of the small houses, a frail man stirred in his sleep. It was morning and a green bird was at the sill of his windowpane singing in an unusual high pitch.

The man frowned and growled in his ethyl sleep, he had been drinking heavily last night: smuggled wine brought by his Jewish neighbors; he pulled the Grey blanket over his head. The bird kept on singing.

"Enough, enough lousy bird, fly away, fly away, before I knock you down…" he shouted in vain.

His mouth was dry and he was having a headache:
"Woman, come in here and bring me my breakfast. What time is it?

A comely woman dressed in the traditional dress of the region came in and said:
"Yes my husband? I was just going to come and wake you up; you came in late last night from your poetry recital."

The man replied angrily:
"Were you that silly green bird?"

"What are you talking about my husband? Please do not be like this, the children will hear. "

The wife pleaded. She knew how callous he could be when he was back from his poetry meetings.

She had brought a tray with a frugal breakfast: some fouls medams, a piece of hot bread and a cup of cinnamon tea.

The man sat on the bed, his beard had grown over the night, and though he was but 40 he looked like a 60 years old man.

The woman's heart grieved: she remembered how alert and gentle he was then, when they first met. Now since he had written some verses, he had become arrogant and unfeeling towards her and the children. Her heart ached deeply but she did not say anything.

The sound of wings was heard the green bird has left the window-pane and had flown away for now. The wife went to open the window.

"Shut the window, woman, I have a migraine and I have to get ready to get to the class. My students are waiting."

Amir was a teacher at the local school, a small-impoverished place owned by the Palestinian education authority where during the hot season he dispensed his classes outdoors. He hated his job nowadays, he was not sure how all this had happened really. Once he loved it with all of his heart.

He had always had big dreams as a boy and most especially since his mother died when he was a young boy. His father has remarried and his second wife was temperamental, he had to prove himself over and over to her in order to keep peace in the household. He would exert acts of childish bravery to catch her attention, make false promises, talk of dreams bigger than reality

His brother had died too during the last war with Israel, and he was left feeling so very alone. So they decided to get him married early, that is as soon as he got a job at the local school and had proved that he could sustain a family of his own.

He had become bored with his married life, with his work he was so tired of the routine. And so he looked at what his mother had left him. He was searching for an illusory treasure but there was nothing much, to his deepest disappointment and anger, nothing of value that he could trade to start a new life.

As he kicked a box out of frustration, some diaries dropped on the floor: they were the poetry books that his elder brother had hand-written. they were unpublished, totally unknown to any living soul.

And so out of boredom he wrote them down and put his name on them. He read them to his pupils, and soon his words were known in the village. They declared him to be talented and, they decided to print the poems at the school press and have them translated in Hebrew.

Nothing much was got from this, but soon he found that the lady teachers were looking at him with a renewed and curious interest. One was a great friend of the Director of the school, she had strong links in Jordan and Palestine, and Egypt, and she was too a poetess.

Slowly he played the same way he had played with his mother in law, and the poetess fell for his gentle and cunning ways. She understood him, and he felt safe. She had suffered enough she narrated to him: during her travels, often she would fall for some Kuwaiti actors who would serenade her and steal her gold at the end of their short-lived affairs.

He knew all that, he did not mind and he named himself Princessloverforever, and started to service her, he called her "possibility"

She fell for his poetic words and she intervened on his behalf so that the school would grant him the use of the only computer they had. She said he would promote Palestinian Poetry, the Poetry of Resistance.

Under village arrest, he discovered the huge world of Internet, and a myriad of "possibilities".

As he taught the class, he felt the beat of the migraine in his left temple and remembered the shrieks of the green bird at his window. He thought: would the green bird ever take him to further shores?

And so thinking, he pressed keys, and went into Yahoo and Hotmail, took different addresses and sent his poetry to ladies of the far away shores of America.

All of the ladies were so much nicer than the ones in the village, they knew how to captivate his curiosity, and they told him of how beautiful and free life was in Washington. When he asked about how they felt about his poetry, they invariably replied:
"Yes, yes Amir it is fine, childish but fine."

And so the next days, the green bird came back sing. Until the day when he called his wife and said:

"Woman go to the school and tell them I am ill, I cannot go to teach today"

The Possibility teacher was very sad, she told the wife:
"Tell him that I will think deeply so that he gets better."

She already knew she had lost him. But she was not angry after all he did not take her gold, yes he borrowed a few hundred dollars, but it was worth it.

The wife has returned with the message, Amir sighed deeply he had grown tired of her, of this life.

And so he sat on his bed, took a piece of paper, and set about to try his hand at poetry and win the attention of the American ladies. And so he penned the Arabian nightmarish Tale, a tale wrong of girls mistreated. They kept asking him how women were treated in Arabia. Yes surely that would please them and win him favors.

It was very wrong to do so, but he was now beyond wrong and right. The green bird came morning after morning to serenade him; he did not mind the high pitch now.

He had emailed the poem to the World authority of Poetry, and the American loved it, yes it fitted so well with their ideas of how life was on the other side of their own traditions.

Amir was crowned that year Poet of the Year, and he won prizes from America. He kept on borrowing money from friends to keep up appearances, to fly left and right in whichever direction the green bird was singing.

Things were going fast, he got drank almost every night, he was tired and filled with despair: the nauseating smell of the words penned wrong prevented him from concentrating-He could no longer keep up with the classes, with the traditional life at the village, the lady teacher was jealous of all his new foreign friends and so she got him fired from his job.

He did not take him long to plan anew, and so he did what he always did, he found a green "possibility" woman, an ugly woman, a poet, back in America: he would go to the Jewish side to find a computer, he did not mind to lose his life on the way, it was so vital for him to follow the green bird, and talk on Messenger to the American woman who was willing to pay for him.

She paid and paid, the green dollars poured over him like rain, and he was brought to her as the green bird flew along side the window of his economy class ticket to New York. He serviced her as he had serviced many before, after all could it be worst that penning the Arabian nightmarish Tale, in full knowledge of the lie?

He finally reached the green side of his life, the dollars and the green card, and he totally forgot the life he used to lead in his village back in Palestine, his wife and children.

He slept with the new possibility, one of many.

The D-Day had come, he had been invited to read in a grand poetry contest, summer 2001, everything was green, and as he stood on the podium of the open stadium he saw wave after wave of human beings. He asked the organizer:

"Sir, who are all those people? It is really a big crowd."

The organizer laughed and replied:
"Well Amir, this is no ordinary crowd those are all potential poets waiting for their green card, this podium is the first step to enter our world. All of them are waiting to take their turn on the stadium; this contest will last for weeks…

As Amir looked on, he found that one woman in the crowd, wearing a white dress, had suddenly stood up and aimed a stone at the green bird. In the distance, he saw the green bird bloody drop dead on the grass.

Israel has just declared war on Palestine.

-The End-

SHORT STORY 20

One French Night in tears

The king had come back from the hunt; a bleeding fawn hung on his white horse. The King was wearing a coy yet triumphant smile; he would celebrate his 25th birthday soon. The King of France was the pride of the France; he was the reflection of the land. He had panache.

His white horse adorned with gold jewels was nervous; the drops of blood running from the prey's wound on his hair were disturbing and he rued his back heels on the marble alley of the Royal Chateau.

Louis knew his horse, and quieted it with a gentle pat between the eyes; he removed one of his gloves, as he did so.

Yet, in the heat of his passion for the horse and the success of his hunt, the royal hunter had forgotten that he was Louis, King of France, and not the mere rider enjoying his victory as he did now. His lackeys were always lost when he was in this mood; they did not dare approach him when he was that happy.

Louis beamed from joy.

As he continued quieting his horse, his right glove fell dry and heavy on the wet ground of the alley. This was a bad omen and it landed ugly in his symbolism in front of the guest from the Orient. Everyone shuddered from fright.

The court, the servants, the marquises, the duchesses, les delicieuses, everyone gasped at the insult that had been laid in front of the foreign guest.

A dark-skinned man curtsied in front of Louis and his horse as he lifted the lambskin white glove of Louis the King of France, and said without raising his eyes:

"My master, the Sultan will meet you Sire, as per customs"

Louis suddenly understood what had happened. But he had barely reached twenty-five years yet his life was nothing but a game of fate: all of it, the hunting, his reign, his days and night, he was not even sure of his own life. A glint of irony came in his eye, knowingly and arrogant. The cardinal of France replied:
"Very well, the duel shall be set later, inform your master."

Louis gingerly stepped down his untamed horse, now curiously calm as if it had understood that life and death were being played in front of it.

The King of France laughed heartily as he walked proudly into the Chateau towards his chambre personnelle.

Tonight was the Menuet soiree, and the clavecin could already be heard throughout the chateau as each guest was arriving in his or her blazoned coach.

Meanwhile, in the left aisle of the Chateau, the court of the foreign visitor was perplexed. Their master had come in good faith.

The Sultan had brought the King of France a magnificent diamond as big as a pigeon's egg; the King had been so pleased. Why this ill luck? Why this bad turn of luck? Why did the astrologer not forewarn the Sultan of this bad omen?

Before starting preparation for the long journey, the Sultan had indeed called in the astrologer and had asked him whether the journey was advisable. After days and nights of calculating the stars' movements, the tired counsel had come and delivered his verdict: The journey to France would bring a great happiness to the Sultan's land and the land of France. The Sultan remembered the way the Counsel 's eyes had become deep with a loving knowledge. The old white bearded man had been by his father as he died. He was one of his most trusted subjects. Has he weakened in his knowledge? After all he was approaching a century, he could barely walk or see. His words were weak and the Sultan had to put his ear close to the old Man.'s mouth to hear his counsel.

His breath was weak yet scented like a mountain rose, words fell from his mouth like soft petals, few and everlasting.

Now, the Sultan was in the land of France. The long journey had been a perilous enterprise; his party had to fight off bandits and rough weather for days. The Sultan was past forty, he had not long to live, he knew that too. He had lived too soon too fast. Recently he had seen in one of his waking dreams the Reincarnation Wheel turn by one link.

From his boyhood, Rushed had been very attracted by the land of France because of the unusual gifts that were brought to his father through the ambassadors of the French kings and chevaliers. They were always ingenious and delightful gifts. He marveled at them for months. He had taken a fancy for the French fashion and had his clothes made in France too.

And so the journey meant a lot to the Sultan.

As they reached the land of France, spring could be felt in the air like some kind of gentle mystical renewal. From his coach, he saw the cornfields bountiful, and the orchard trees blooming with rainbows of flowers. And when at last, his party reached the King of France Chateau, he was shocked by the refinement of the monuments, the intricacy of the architecture, the mirrors, and the gentle music and laughter all around the place.

His life back at home felt sad in comparison. There was so many restrictions put on him because of his rank. He did not remember hearing such laughter. He felt a sharp pain in his heart, like an absence, an endurable absence; a deep longing that his soul was unable to express.

The Court of France had ordered a Menuet Night and invitations for that dainty feast had been sent to many foreign lords. The Sultan had been so pleased when he had received the Lys scented message from the French Court. Immediately, the French ambassador had arranged for a tutor to teach the Sultan, the Menuet's steps. Those were delightful dance steps and the Sultan learnt quickly.

Now, because of a mere glove, the sultan 's heart was heavy with a duty of honor he could not possibly avoid. Tears run down his cheeks.

On the other side of the Chateau, the French King was happily singing in his powder room as the courtiers were fixing his wig and face powder.

At the sound of the French King's youthful song, the sharp pain of the uncertain absence to come once again pierced the heart of the Sultan.

Louis was admiring himself in the long mirror in his Chambre Personnelle and was happy as young Narcissus, at the reflection of his elegant silhouette. Beautiful ribbons had been tied in his hair, knees, shoes, and coat sleeves.

The music coming from the grand ballroom was entrancing. The best musicians from Vienna were in the employ of the Court of France. They knew the taste of young Louis for the Clavecin and the gentle dances.

Louis 'entrance was announced with great zeal. He had promised the dance to his cousin, a lovely and witty girl. And Louis danced his 25 years old away in the steps of the menuet, without a care, enamoured with the reflections of his figures in the gold vessels of the court hall. The ribbons looked ravishing like butterflies wings. He whirled the girl away into the arms of another dancer, she was too talkative, and he had grown tired already.

Louis's heart was longing to walk in the Gallery Des Mirroirs back in Versailles. Mirrors and his own reflections had always obsessed him, he was infatuated by the narcissist fathom that he saw in his private galleries. He talked to his reflections, he danced with them, he cried at them.

Chambord was but a past time, where he met other dignitaries, and rode the newest horses. It was pleasant but Versailles was indeed his favorite. The only curtsey he truly loved was the one he gave himself in front of his own silent mirror.

The Sultan had arrived in the Dance hall dressed in silk pantalons and vest, embroidered with jewels, at forty the Sultan was indeed looking very handsome. In many ways he outshined the King of France. And Louis took an instant dislike to the man. He did care to hide it either, this was his chateau and his land, and he could do as he very well pleased.

Louis ' Court was embarrassed by this unexpected rivalry, yet the Sultan through his gentle manners brought them close to him, as he started to dance the Menuet with une delicieuse de Ramblais. The couple was exquisite in their refined steps.

Louis' attention was already elsewhere.

The Sultan in his heart felt a great Love for Louis de France. He saw how healthy a man he was, so carefree, so elegant. He could not but admire what Louis had made of the Court of France, a magical island.

The king and he had but a few hours before dawn, and the duel. The matter had already been resolved; they would use the mousquetier, a firearm. It would be fast and one of them would have to lose his life.

Louis' hatred of the Sultan increased, as the Court of France grew fonder of the gentle stranger. His foreseeable tragic fate had added to his mystic aura.

Louis ' glare was focused on a new vessel. A gold timbale encrusted with flawless diamonds which captured Louis image and reflected it manifold in challenging arrows to the crystals chandeliers of the Court of France, it outshined every other vessel. Louis was mesmerized.

This fascination did not go unnoticed by the Sultan. The vessel was a personal gift from him to Louis. Was the King of France aware of this? The Sultan did not want to answer this question.

Time was going fast. The court was already withdrawing, the hours had evaporated like mere seconds, and everyone made way for the exit of the King of France.

There was a cold shift felt throughout the dance room, as the queen and her lady of waiting left for another wing of the Chateau. Louis had not even cared to bow to the First Lady of France, as he had been consummated by hatred for the Stranger. He behaved arrogantly like a spoilt adolescent.

Louis's mind was no more in Ramblais; it was back in Versailles, in his fairy gallery, back to the mirrors and the delicious hours he spent enamoured by his reflections.

In the Sultan's quarters, everyone felt gloomy. The Sultan was reputed to be an excellent shooter. He was very swift. They had no doubt that the Sultan would overpower the young king of France.

The Sultan was strangely quiet and relaxed now inspite of the dark mood around him. He had just spent the most marvelous night of his life, the Menuet Night. He had no care or no fear now, he just knew that the fate was indeed with him. He had understood the meaning of the Menuet Steps. An exact trail in the human destiny. He was ready for the duel. Louis was easily captured by a dazzle. He was no match to him, he knew that already. It would be very easy to distract him and strike him to death.

In the morning, 6am, when the dew was still on the grass leaves, two carriages arrived. The King of France's and the Sultan's.

Witnesses were not standing by, neither the Sultan nor Louis were agitated. A single shot was heard, and a body falling heavy on the ground. Wailing mounted in the spring morning of France, it was a loud wailing of the orient and not the quiet moans of the West; the Sultan was dead, a bullet in his heart. His hands empty, he had not even touched his gun.

Hastily his body was taken back to the carriage, Louis smiled.

An hour ago, an agreement had been passed, unknown to the courts of France or of the Sultan's.

The Sultan went to see Louis and told him how he wished to die in the Menuet's night. He felt it was his destiny to depart from life in the Menuet steps. He wanted to be buried in the Menuet Night.

And so Louis felt the anguish of this special man, he felt the charisma of the sultan's soul and he acquiesced.

As the carriage of the Sultan left the land of France in mourning, in the coffin the corpse of another had been laid to be taken back to the East.

While in the king's carriage galloping back to Versailles. Louis was seated besides the limp corpse of the Sultan. Within the next few hours, a magical grave would be built behind the mirror gallery of Versailles.

The Herald was shouting a new decree of the Court, Menuet nights would be held in La Gallerie Des Miroirs at Versailles, not any more in

Ramblais or Chambord. They could be held nowhere else but in Versailles' Galleries Des Mirroirs.

The prophecy of the old astronomer proved true, as Louis spent most of his nights in Versailles' galleries Des Miroirs, thus honoring the Sultan with his presence, more often than any other soul had been by a King of France. And the Sultan's soul watched over the reflections of the King of France, so that no ill-omens or bad spells would taint the image of Louis, albeit through the mirrors of death.

The Menuet Night lasted by a 1000 lifetimes.

-The End-

SHORT STORY 21

No Woman No Cry

It has been raining now for forty days and more now over African land. Everything was wet; everything was decaying floating on the surface of the rancid water. Corpses and belongings. Some new wailing was heard in the distance, a newborn had died of the water disease: Al Maya.

It was August in Addis Ababa. On the land of Ethiopia, There had been drought for years, people had from generation to generation prayed from drops of rain to come and soothe their parched throats.

It was so eerie. Doctors were prepared like every year for droughts and relief agencies had sent as usual the normal medicines to fight dehydration. Since forty days, it had been raining, inundating huts and palaces alike, the infants had always-new diseases, worms that grew in their body. Malaria killed the eldest.

Since forty days, it had been raining heavily, inundating huts and palaces alike, the infants were contracting new diseases, worms that grew so tall in their bodies. Malaria killed the eldest.

It continued raining heavily, storms and lightening flashed angrily in the low and dark sky of Africa. None could leave or come in that land any longer, it was like a Black Sea cut off from the rest of the world.

A dying land taken in the grips of fate, that none could undo.

Old people were dying fast too, women, and only a group of young African was still surviving, those in the prime of their life.

They had put the blame on the oldest for invoking the Rain Goddess through tribal cries and dances, and Voodoo. And so when the flood came, and the elder died, they left them unburied, carried down by the angry gush of dark waters.

Soon all the infants and old people were dead.

There was no let up in the downfall; soon everyone was terrified, having to face the loneliest of death. Huge snakes and rats were entering the palaces looking for new preys; they were fat and strong.

There was but a dozen young man, a woman, the ruler and 2 lions in the only dry room of the land. They eyes were red with fright, the rats and the snakes were feeding noisily on the corpses and any living prey outside their door.

The two lions were couched on the marble floor, intoxicated by the rancidity of the inside air.

One young man asked the Ruler, a younger man with an arrogant face:

Your highness, there is not much to eat, it would be best to let one lion go"

The ruler shouted:
Shut up, ignorant, those are my Lions, they will protect me.

The young man bowed his head and replied:
Yes, your majesty, but when the food will be short and we shall not be able to feed the lions, surely they will eat us.

The ruler shrieked louder:
Shut up, I have spoken and my will shall be done.

The young man went on his knees and cried
Yes Your Majesty, this is your will, please forgive me for I should listen to your wisdom

The ruler closed his eyes; the words thus spoken to him reminded him of the words I had spoken long ago when he was a child.

It was so long ago. He remembers his grandfather The Lion Heart of Africa. He remembers him well walking in the street of London, an unknown person to many there, but one that took long training to come back and free his country from the Italians.

His grandfather was called the Lion Heart, he remembers that. But he looks so frail while in London. He would stand up when British would call on him. Before scheduled meetings, he would rehearse his lines never like an ill-prepared actor. But again, he remembered too how the British ordered him to do this and that.

And then explain to his son, his father who died not so long ago too in a French car accident, that the Italian were the worst, he would put up with the arrogance of the British.

As the days passed in London, his grandfather was becoming awesome, they would call him Your Highness, and it would feel right. He then ordered other as if everyone was his slave. He remembers all the white women coming in and out the beauty queens, the drunken nights.

His father too led a dissolute life, and his aunts were wearing western dresses and laughed at other women of the land, calling them primitive, his grandmother was withdrawn and hurt, she did not speak much any longer. Too much was going on.

Then time came to go back to the African Land, and he was put on a throne high, the boy remember how he was made the Emperor, and the day Italian troops withdrew. His grandfather was elated. He had won.

But soon the British were coming fewer to him; other leaders were busy with their own affairs in their own lands. And he was bored of his subjects.

He traveled again, visited a few other countries. Came home and realized he was not loved. Those other rulers were treated with such refined protocol. So he called on his scribes and told them that from now on,
They would have to revise the protocol.

The British came back with frowned face. There was a blackman without a name, who sang some pretty hard songs against the white.

His name was rob Barley. He had a natural magnetism and he was start-ing to draw crowds. A Jamaican. Ahhhh they were not happy at all.

So they said: do whatever, promise him the moon and the stars, and let him play in your pawn.

His grandfather said: Yes, I shall but in return I want to be respected like a God

The British laughed. Yes, of course whatever. Declare yourself as such we shall manage it our side. No problem.

That night, everything was arranged, and soon Reggae music was heard in the vast rooms of the palace, the raucous voice of the Jamaican singer. It spoke of poverty and ganja.

It was a powerful music. Soon, the little boy listened along with the other members of the family all of the songs of the Jamaican singer. Grandfather smiled inwardly a coy smile and said: he will do perfectly.

And so an envoy was sent to Jamaica. The meetings were arranged. Yes Rob would be the emissary of a new Ah of Ethiopia, a perfect arrangement. Money was plenty now in the pocket of the poor singer. Money, ganja, clothes, new equipment.

He arrived in Ethiopia, concerts were arranged. Ah, Ah is the light the mass chanted hypnotized by this lean black man.

And Ah became the One.

None was allowed to approach him but the singer and the British's. They would free Africa from slavery.

And soon Ah traveled to London and other western cities, taking with him the emissary the singer. Even the white mass loved him, money poured in for Ah.

The singer was happy, he had no cares any longer, he was full, his time was full, and he had everything he wanted, the miss beauty contests, the ganja even on British soil, everything.

Ah and he returned to Ethiopia, where the followers acclaimed them.

Ah had become envious of the singer, none acknowledged him as they did that wretched and dirty singer of Jamaica.

One night one shotgun was fired towards the singer, he did not die.

But he had to leave, Ah commanded, for his safety.

Ah had then everything he wanted, he was Ah, and he had lions as his best friend. Sedated lions, they impressed the public when they came, for none dared to come near.

Ah had forgotten his wife of before his endowment as Ah, and the black woman cried a river. He sneered at her and sang: No Woman, No Cry.

She said: Women's tears will flow long and hard on your land, Ah. Make it stop.

Ah laughed and said: You are insane woman, do not come in my presence any longer

And it was the last the little boy saw of his grandmother.

The singer was in London, he developed a brain cancer, and he was still having a grand life in the prison of his illness, he begged to come to Africa to die,

Meanwhile, the erudite class of Ethiopia, the students sneered too at the false idol, and a Coup d'Etat was staged successfully. Ah had to feel to Britain.

In Jamaica, the black love of the singer cried and they sneered at her: no woman no cry, he has a miss beauty contest.

Tears kept flowing in pure hearts.

Both the men died in exile. There is but one grand son to understand the play and the stages, he witnessed some of the acts
No, he knew that the flood was the woman's revenge.

And so he declared:
May that woman be given as food to my lion, kill her and feed her to my lions they will protect me for I am the descendant of Ah, he is coming for me.

The men did as he said.

The lion were peaceful for the day, but as the night came, they became crazed by the hissing of the water rats and snakes, and remembered how gentle they felt when they ate human flesh, and so the Lion Kings ate up the last of the Ah dynasty.

No Woman No cry, the flood stopped, Africa was a beggar, but not a slave any more.

The rainbow will shine again, frightening away the rats of pain and the snakes of revenge.

Africa was a beggar but no more a slave.

-The End -

SHORT STORY 22

The Stage Costume

The finale had been magnificent; the audience has stood up to give the main character the ovation she deserved

The role the actress had just played was a complex role, and few if none could act it out as well as she did, it was almost like a scene taken from the tradition of the Comedia Dell'Arte, with little words, with subtle meanings expressed solely through the movements, the fluidity of the actress's poses.

The plot was simple, almost a replica of Romeo and Juliet, except that here Juliet was the absolute main role.

The director had been working on a tight budget from the very beginning, and he had chosen her among hundreds of applicants who were ready to tour the south of France.

She had been on such low budget tours and, she was fully aware of how hard, how taxing it could be on anyone's life. But she had always come through those, undisturbed, unchanged. It did not really matter.

Anataalie was a young actress of twenty-two, she had finished her acting classes only a year ago She was tall, slender with delicate limbs, her skin was milk and roses, her hair was natural chestnut, long and wavy...her eyes were brown and fiery, there was a fragility and beauty about her that made anyone who looked in her fiery eyes trapped in her stare.

When she came to the audition, the stage manager, the director saw the hundreds of applicants but they had noticed her among them all, there was that something in her that spoke immediately to the minds and the hearts of people.

She sat in the last row of the audition room. And watched as actors and actresses were being auditioned. The director was nervous, annoyed, he systemically expedited each new audition. Anataalie already knew that he was anxious to audition her.

Her name was called:
"Mademoiselle Anataalie"

As she climbed to the stage, her step light likes a ballerina a series of calculated moves; an attentive silence reigned suddenly over the place. She started acting: everyone stared at her, she recited the lines, offered the gestures, and the moves. She looked at none, strangely surreal her wide open eyes seemed to look inwards

The director's heart had already deciphered the meaning she held for him.... He let her carry on, whilst he had cut short every other audition before the 3 minutes were elapsed, for over an hour. She did not seem mind or to tire, she continued to act her role.

Then the director climbed to the stage and declared:
" Natalie, you are on."

She replied:
"Thank you"

And left the stage without giving a second look at the director.

The stage manager told her to come back after two days to finalize the contract, and get her role manuscript.

On the appointed date, she came had done earlier. Without a word. The stage manager gave her the main role part; she did not seem to care. The old man tried to read her face but there was nothing there for him, and he resigned himself to being none but a manager of stage props, he felt a little blue.

As she looked into the manuscript, the stage manager added that he had been given specific instructions to indulge her every whim in regards to costumes. She looked inwardly and recoiled. She had not time for frills and petty talks.

She said:
"Thank you. But the role I have been given is the main part. And it is indeed the part of the heart, the heart has no costume, So I would like to wear on stage a fluid cotton dress of French blue."

The stage manager became perplexed:
"But, Mademoiselle, it is the main role, surely you would want something more elaborate. "

She replied:
"No. You told me that I could choose, as I wanted, I chose."

She played the part every night in many towns of France, it was a success every where. They had come full circle and were now back in Paris.

Tonight was the Grand Finale, all of Paris was there standing on their feet, offering her a loud ovation with shouts of encore…everyone loved her.

She had played the part so well for the last two months, she had worn the same simple dress, yet she looked magnificent, she had no make up on at all, her hair were loose long to her waist. For the last few weeks, she had become the queen of all the art reviews; they called her the best ever.

She did not read those, the other actors and actresses talked about it, but she did not reply, she did not mix with others, and everyone had become accustomed to her aloofness.

In every performance, she had been playing her own heart, Juliet, and she could bring tears and sobs at will, tears were rolling down her cheeks, she could bring a blush to her cheek when she recited the love lines, she would become so pale and fragile when she recited the lines of a lost love. Her body would become so tiny, so fragile, it was incredible…She is a natural they wrote about her.

No props, no make-up, she was the ultimate actress.

Tonight was her finale, and she curtsied to the adoring audience, bouquet after bouquet of roses and flowers were thrown on the stage. The run was over; it was the last day for this drama, her performance would continue to haunt many hearts, so they wrote in many magazines.

She sat in her lodge, relieved, it was all over.

There was a gentle knock on the door, the director asked:
"Anataalie, may I come in?"

She did not reply she was changing her costume stage, the plain blue dress into her own dress, a burgundy velour dress. The director gasps at her loveliness in the gorgeous dress.

He continued:
"There we are Anataalie, this was indeed a grand finale. I came to tell you that I have written a new play and I want you as my main actress."

Anataalie did not reply.

He said:
" Anataalie, this is the finale but I need to see you again for you have become a part of me. You know so well how to convey the impulses of my words to the public. It feels as if you have opened my heart and read all of its contents".

Anataalie remained silent.

The Director felt pain in his heart:
"Anataalie, you are haunting me, you have got to give me a sound from your heart"

She did not reply

The Director checked himself, knowing already that this battle he had already lost:

"Will you be my main actress? Let us start the rehearsal from tomorrow"

She did not reply

The broken voice of the director continued speaking words:

"Anataalie, I cannot live without you, please if you cannot love me, then let me love you close or from afar, do not refuse my love"

She turned her head, and then he saw that tears inundated her face: "No"

She walked away and he never saw her again this close.
He went to all her opening nights; she never worked more than once with any one director. . She was a very talented actress and the audience adored her" Anataalia they would call, more, encore, encore, encore!

Every night, after the soiree, she would hail a taxi, and go to that place she called her home, a lovely apartment in the bourgeois Paris.

The maid would welcome her:
"Good morning Mademoiselle Anataalie"

She would say
"How is Roman today, please tell me quickly".

Today the maid replied as always:
"He is fine, he slept well but he has had another crisis, he asked for you several times"

Anataalie climbed the stairs as fast as she could and entered the bedroom.

The room was airy and beautifully decorated; there was a bed with four columns. A young man was lying among the pure white bed sheets. His face was emaciated and pale.

She said:
"Romain, how was the night."

He said:
"I dreamt of a beautiful place. Please Anataalie, play your act of today exactly as you played it."

She replied:
"But yes of course Romain, let me put my costume stage."

She went to the next room, and chose a new costume, a wonderful garment of silk embroidered with gold thread and swarowsky crystal, a princess dress, of extreme beauty.

She wore it, and put on her rubies and diamond necklace, the one he liked best,
She looked at herself in the mirror and loved the magical reflection, and she was indeed a Parisian beauty.

She went into Romain's room; a faint smile came on his pale face as he saw her enter. She was so beautiful.

He said:
"Anataalie, do go on. Do not make me wait."

And she re-enacted tonight finale, he was enthralled by her beauty and talent.

She felt tired, but she did not show it to him, she would never show him how she truly felt, how cold she had felt in her heart for the last few months.

She remembered so well, oh so very well, that terrible day, when the doctor called and told her:

" Romain has aids, he does not have long to live…"

. She had collapsed in the doctor's room:

" Doctor, she cried, surely, you can give me some hope, there must be something we can do"

The doctor said:

"No, Anataalie, there is nothing anyone can do. Just do the best you can to make him comfortable."

The despair in her was total, her entire life flashed in her mind, her dreams, her hopes, her past, her future. Everything had become meaningless now. She had wanted to die then and there.

Tonight she re-played the finale, just for him. As she finished she came close to Romain, caressed his hair and said:

"This is the finale for this play, but I have signed up for another one though."

He smiled at her.

Then she said:

"Romain, you must sleep now, take your sedatives and medications, she brought the glass to his lips and helped him take his medicines. He looked so happy.

Then she bent over him, and put a soft kiss on his forehead and said:

"Sleep well brother, when you dream, please dream of mother, she loves you so very much."

He replied:
"Yes, sister, I will. I will also tell her that you are growing as beautiful as she was when I meet her soon. She was my favorite actress, and you are my second favorite actress.

He laughed softly. She stayed until he was asleep and went to her room.

-The End-

Short Story 23

The vows of silence

It was 4am in the morning, in the Ashram of the countryside of England. It was cold, and the hens and roosters were sending the dawn the usual wake up call in a strident symphony.

The animal world in the sheds of the Ashram was slowly awaking, rising up from the sitting pause of the profound death of the night while men were still lying flat on their back, so vulnerable, in the duality of their mortal life. The animal world was too raising on their limbs, after the half closed sleep of a their unprotected state always threatened by predators and the butcher knife alike…The seat of slaughter, the bed of the murder was indeed the night of the spiritual awakened life

Slowly, shivering silhouettes in saffron cover emerged from the darkened house holding in their hand the galvanized buckets, and soon each silhouette was busy taking away the booty from each animal family, eggs and milk, bringing it back to the darkened lodge

Soon a gong was heard, a loud, compact and oppressed sound. And lights were switched on, dimmed by the emerging day.

Everyone, young men with shaven skulls and fat women, and children with hair still undone by sleep came limply to the middle of the yard, and they assembled around the bricked well. One matron lady began to push the pump and a flow of water stated flowing rhythmically... All of them took some water in the cup of their hands and washed hurriedly they sleepy faces; the impact of the cold water made their skin flush crimson at once in the bite of the frozen water.

Some had simple Kashmir shawls of dull Grey or brown draped over their body like a blanket, the little ones were kept close to the thighs of the mothers enveloped under the pangs of the shawl, we could see only a little pair of blue eyes and the tiny toe nails coming from under the shawls emerging from the regular leather sandals with one strap on the big toe-nail...

Soon the thirty-eight members had finished their morning ablutions and returned to the lodge one by one, like a slow train starting in an empty and Grey faded station.

The older women stopped pumping, and locked the pump with a key, which brutal silver glint clashed with the soft saffron color of her outfit.

Everyone else was sitting in the meditation room; their throat dry from the long night sleep...they waited like cattle would wait for their shepherd to take them to the flush grass and graze in giddy acceptance.

It was very cold and as the matron came in, she switched off the light. She closed the door, and switched on the electric heater...She then designated two helpers and told them to follow her to the kitchen.

The kitchen had a barren look except for the recently brought in baskets of eggs and the buckets full with the steaming warm milk of the cows, which had been left on the wooden table.

A huge pan of water was boiling on the stove, and soon the matron added to it some rose waterish fluid and a rose from a vase of which she tore mercilessly its petals and threw them in the pan of boiling water. The kitchen soon was filled with a fragrant vapor.

Meanwhile, the helpers had put a ladder in the buckets of milk, and were frying the eggs, adding some slice of bananas and apples in the batter.

The gong sound was heard for the second time this morning, and the matron, poured the petal rosewater, still steaming over into silver bowl already half filled with cold water, and put a thermometer in it. Yes, it was at the right temperature. She checked her hair in the reflection of the water, she was fine; then she took a fresh ivory towel with initial YM and carried the silver bowl into the meditation room, the helpers opened the door and proceeded with the morning procession. They entered the main room.

In the higher seat, which was set on a raised platform and decorated with cushions of Asian workmanship, carpets and garlands of flower, was a motionless man in a yogi lotus posture? His legs crossed on the seat, the sole of his feet in touch with his open palms. He was obese, his hair was jet black, long, and thin, so was his beard. He too wore a saffron suit but of heavier material, and he had around him a white shawl embroidered with gold leaves… His eyes were closed; he seemed to be in a trance. The matron gently went besides him, and said:

"Guru, here is the water as she proceeded to put it on a rosewood table besides him."

He slowly opened his eyes, dipped his little finger into the water, yes the temperature was right. He nodded his head, and the matron ordered the two helpers to raise the silver bowl Slowly the guru put his head into the water and opened his eyes into the water several times, inhaling some water too. Then he raised his head and circulated the rose petal water into his nostrils and put his head again deep into the water this time releasing the water through the left nostril, reopening his eyes and swallowing the water. Once more he raised his head, gargled the rose water and went again into the silver basin and reopened his eyes and released the gargled water. His purification ritual was over for now.

Everyone seated at his feet further down watched the morning ritual, and each day they felt the same calmness coming over them. In their shivers, they followed the course of the warm water on the respected guru beard.

The journey of the warm water on the guru face was in itself a soothing fairy tale in their cold flesh. They felt with him the sootiness of the warm water…it was hypnotic…everyone floated above their humane condition, out of their mortal body and was reaching to the elusive warmth of that watery journey…

Then the Guru started the Mantra, and for one hour the walls of the lodge resounded with the mantra chanting, a piercing chant that was disquietening to the animal worlds as the cows, the hens, the birds were responding with shrieking sounds…

The gong once again rang, and the helper brought out the milk and the eggs curry and each one was served on a banana leaf on the floor, and each one drank directly from the ladder the fresh milk still warm…

This was no ritual, they dispensed with it rapidly, the guru never ate with them, he simply watched over, noone ever saw him eat, noone knew where he ate or whether he ate at all, but all that they saw is that his cheeks were plump and his body obese.

The gong rang once again with a new severity.

The guru spoke in a muted voice and said to the devotees: "Today is the day where one is to concentrate on silence, and so today none is to speak a syllable or a word.

If you do, you shall be penalized and left without food for a week. Everyone is under this duty except for children below five years old.

The duty was set, and a deadly silence set on the lodge, only disquieting animal sounds were still heard from afar.... Everyone went on doing his her own duty, gardening, studying, not a sound was heard...

Today was the day of the washing of the saffron suits and all the women were to go to the well and pump the water one by one.... It was a good duty, it allowed them to keep busy and their blood running in their veins thus keeping their body warm. Today was indeed a very cold day...

So they brought buckets with rough soap cubes and stones for removing the hardest stains on the clothes, and started the hard duty. Their hands soon were bluish from cold, and steam was seen floating away from their nostrils. With every breath, some of the warmth was taken away from them. They felt colder, so they washed harder. It was so very cold.

There was no noise the children who were out there were between five and seven years old and they knew that it would be not good to talk, they did not utter a sound. They were well trained. They looked like sad puppets

Everyone worked in silence and contemplation, trying to forget the cold that was biting their fingers. The water was so cold.

Soon the task was nearly over and the women went to hang the loads of wet clothes on the lines between the tall and lean trees. There was no noise, the birds were frightened, and sounds of wings flying away were heard as they came closer at regular intervals or the sounds of squirrels running away, climbing away from them, high in the trees. The dry autumn's leaves cracked under their steps. It was 9am and in the sky heavy white and grayish clouds hid the sun.

As they were hanging the clothes, one of the woman Radian looked around to see if her children were still close, yes Anju and Raju were with her, helping out with stern little faces. But she did not see Pradeeb....she looked everywhere he was nowhere to be found...She did not talk, the Guru's order was sacred and so she left everything and run to the well, she had a feeling, a bad feeling...

There he was, the five years old little blond boy with blue eyes, the adventurer they called him...He had turned the bucket upside down and had climbed on it next to the open well. Rajuna wanted to call his name and make him look her way, but the Guru did ordain that today, no word should be spoken aloud, if the vow of silence was broken for any reason, bad things would happen. If she called out, maybe that bad thing would be...

No she did not want to think about it now, she could not think clearly, it was best to follow the Guru's order. The vow of silence was indeed a sacred order, he was known in the Ashram as the only man of wisdom, he was above everyone else, he was worshipped like a deity.

She run, tears running down her cheeks, she saw him through the veil of her tears. She felt herself spiritually struggling: should she break her vow of silence, should she disobey? If she broke the vow of silence, surely something bad would happen.

She could not think, she was so torn as she saw her beautiful child Pradeeb put his little leg over into the void of the well.

Should she call, scream, break the vow of silence? Her mind raced so fast, she could not think so clearly: if she did the Guru said something bad would happen, and she did not utter a word…

She saw the second tiny leg go into the void, she felt herself running so fast to stop that step in death..

…It was too late, the little boy has fallen into the well, she saw him falling like a sad tiny puppet which strings had been cut unexpectedly, he had not screamed either, he had not uttered a sound…The Guru had ordained the vow of silence.

She stayed there all day, none missed her, and it was the day of the Vow of Silence. Everyone was staying lonely in different spots of the area, to avoid meeting the other for fear that somehow to be close to another could spark a sound, a start of a discussion, of a greeting.

Rajuna did not utter a word; she just sat there.

Then in the evening, all assembled into the meditation room and the Guru came in a similar fashion to supervise over the evening meals and the mantra chanting.

When this was over, the gong resounded in the mansion, and he started talking, he said you see how easy was the Vow of Silence, our house shall be protected from evil for some time, because the word is all powerful…Refraining from talking today did save us from evil.

As they sat to eat and talk as usual, he saw that Rajuna did not speak, her face was downcast and she did not eat. He chided Rajuna in a harsh voice:
"Rajuna, do not try to be better than others, the vow of silence is over, speak, speak now"

…She did not reply, no words could come out, all the words in her had died then. She got up and went to pack her few belongings and left without a word, never to come again to the Ashram,

The next morning the Guru came in his usual fashion, undisturbed, and proceeded with ordaining the affairs of the day. As he did, he concluded by stating:
"Yesterday was the day of silence, we know that RaJuna has left because she did not obey me, she cried. The crying is a wording in itself, it was very wrong of her. As she let her tears talk, the little boy was trapped in her own selfishness and disobedience to me: evil did come and took away the little boy to death earlier that he would have if she had obeyed me. A cry, a tear is a word, make no mistake there. He died; she brought this upon herself…now here are the new instructions…"

His voice lost in the wind that blew outside the mansion.

Rajuna was already away so far away, this was the last place she had been where her voice had been heard, it was indeed a tomb in the real life, a sin. She had paid a heavy price and will pay the price everyday. No word will be spoken from her as her final punishment upon living in the tomb of reality; she understood it all now. The Vow of Silence was her life, only in death she would be allowed to speak again the words of truth, the words of her heart freed from the clutch of others' selfish ambitions and giddy acceptance.

-The End-

POETRY OF FUTURISM

The Temptress
The temptress lies alone
As the tale of her seduction
Unfolds in silk vapors

Enveloping the mould
Of the earth,
To prevent another stillborn...
She talks fiercely
In volcanoes, of the ecstasy in life
And in rivers cold, of the chilling lust
Of the full moons
The scarlet flowers in her eyes
Dip nonchalantly in the salty tears
Of the barefooted orphans
Who shine the shoe of poetry?
The heavy tresses
Left in her lap by a rebel monk
Bind the book of the truly unique
Hallway of eternity:
Thy prayer.

THE MAGIC MAN
The star studded
Dark blue night
Shined
Over a garden
Weaned
Like
An Ispahan carpet

In its turquoise heart,
A lady attired in silk vapors
And rainbow dust
Sat quietly,
Her eyes closed.

The shadow
Of her eyelashes
Was her only veil?

A magic man had stopped
In her night.
Mesmerized
By her fragile beauty

He started giving promises
Of a mortal paradise
That could be hers,
Now
If she would only look
At him

He would make flowers
Bloom
Even in winter
He would alight a day
In any darkness.

She did not move.

At dawn,
When the magic man was
Out of words

She opened her eyes
And told him
With an heavenly sigh
That brushed
Away
Yet another mirage:

You were but
Tale 611
And
She flew away,
On the garden carpet
Toward the next night
Leaving behind
The magic man tied
By the seven knots
Of Mortal Life

Do not tear the night sky
My quill refuses to write there is no more ink in my heart
I watch the last summer birds fly away
We have no words to say to each other
Please do not tear the night sky

The gentle moon lays offered like a parchment
Pierrot the clown had a sad face; the candle is no more
Another promise walking further away
Please do no tear the night sky

My words refuses to be moved from their place
In the sun, they felt the sand under their feet of lead
They still whisper some beautiful dreams in my ear
Please do not tear the night sky.

Give me time to be swallowed by nature
Let me make sense of the end in my hand
Of one blue sky, which they said, was limitless
Please do not tear the night away

Good-bye
Before I make you go away.
Give me time to rehearse your farewell
I want to do it right, I want to play it well

Perhaps I could make a list of my best lines
Or play short and long and pick
The winning twig to the best good bye

My words are impatient,
We have come to the end of that page
Where I cannot even call you a friend,
I may let you hide in my smile for a while
I may let you close yours eyes over my lies.

Walk away from me, I will turn my back
On you if you want. Will it make it any easier on you?
Please do not go crying in the rain again.
I told you it was a waste, and very silly too
Why cannot you do what I do each time?
Narrow it down to a little joke. Put everything
You loved about me: my wits and my charm
Into the shape of a zero, nil zips and magnifies the rest.
Good-bye

The snowman
In that place he only knows,
The walls feel like a womb, warm and safe
There is no sunset or sunrise
To remind him of a name he wants no more

The life yet to be is ushered away, unwelcomes.
That is where he wants to spend his days
In the softness of the night

Yet, his heart twinkles when a thought of me visits him
He pens out rhyme after rhyme to deafen the heartbeat
In his chest, ripped open by a good bye.

Pretend that you did not see it.
I will take the snow in the farewell and make
A snowman with a carrot as his nose
I will stay besides the snowman and make him feel
The fire of Africa, and the blazing forest, it will melt away
The snowman of my goodbye is gone. Come out and see.
Please, do not hurt.

The Capuchins
At dusk, the capuchins
Walk through the walls of silence
Tripping over a ground made weak
By the burden of a prayer no longer
Sang away by the opium-fed masses.

The chalice wears the roughest hair shirt
A mad race to humiliation, a trance lying
On three hard boards
Where are the sheep? Where is the wolf?

The weight of human ego broke
The existentialist wheel into a flat ground
Four columns of monks to keep the roof
Of a pagan ritual, vertical and haughty.

Ecstasies of the soul are left to fend for themselves
In a confessional omission.
Cells of stones drowned in nihilism.
A bell keeps ringing deep in human conscience
The smelling salt of the sublime is few

CAIN'S DREAM

The tarnished Word sees
Through the single eye of Cain's grave
The blinding illusion of tomorrows
Like a blanket of snow, the white sky
Lies further south of the soul
Along the awakened sighs
Of the wronged and the weak

One book left unbent yet unread
For the sake of an escape
Within the womb that longs to breathe
Yet, in the final resting-place.

Copyrighted Rahman,brigitte arlette

Epilogue

Those writings are a few among thousands, perhaps in this lifetime they shall be published. I cannot tell now. They spring from a pure source and try to show you the signs within life that will help you survive the overmen among us,

Afterword

I had wanted to write in my own local language, rather than to get it editor razor sharp, the imagery is what is most important in my visions. Believe it or not all the above are part of realities I lived

Conclusions

Over to the other side of Big Ben

The roads of Earl Court's London were all empty, it was snowing heavily, and the cold was humid and very damp.... It was New Year day, and the city had a desolate look about it... there were some remnants of festivity, some empty less champagne bottles, some Christmas tree decoration strewn over the street, Grey and lifeless.... The Big Ben had rang meticulously midnight and the revelers were all home, happy to have made one useful wish, to keep them dreaming and hoping for one more year till next new year's eve. Everything was as it should be...for a New Year's morning in London.

It was so cold, none was out... yet a long white limousine was cruising the roads, and stopped by the Earl's Court's tube station.... The car looked like a polar bear with red eyes, in the foggy morning...a surreal sight, the windows were dark, and none could see inside...

It parked there for 10 minutes, and then a driver in uniform came out and opened the door of the car.... A tall elegant lady in a long white mink coat and high heels stepped out.... She wore a Russian mink cap too, white.... She fitted the scene so well... the collar of the mink was closed high neck and only her fiery brown eyes could be seen...

She was tall and very steady, she walked assuredly on the slippery pavement, the driver anxiously watched her go, and stood next to the limousine, shivering in his uniform...he followed her with his eyes, with utmost respect...and yet his anguish was palpable...but he did not move.

It was a sight so out of the ordinary, and yet nothing seemed amiss in this scene. The white limousine parked in the dirty damp street, deserted by the revelers at 4 am in the morning, the beautiful woman walking alone without escort, seems quite natural.... It felt as if it was a rehearsal to a scene done over and over again...Each of her steps was silent and exact, there was no hesitation in her steps, in her movement, in her body, in her stare.

She walked straight towards the entrance of the tube station, the gates were open but no entry were permissible to the train station itself...As she approached the gates, faces started to show, dirty faces, dazed faces, ugly faces, bodies crawling on the cold concrete floor of the station.... Some did not move, just opened their eyes in amazement, in drunken stupor...

Some drunk told her, go home doll, the time to take the train is over...come back after 2 hours.... None cared...she walked and looked around...she did not respond, some touched her mink, she did not move, she looked at all the faces with her fiery eyes...everyone was under the spell of the tall beautiful lady, who walked in a trail of her favorite scent the Blue Yves Saint Laurent Rive Gauche perfume. She had no bag; her hands were in the sleeves of the mink coat, Cossack fashion like.

She stood in the middle of them and started looking at each of them one by one... one asked her:

"Who are you?"

She said:
"Not your business,"
Her tone was soft and yet cruelly sharp.

Then slowly she turned her around and walked away back to the limousine.
The driver straightened himself, opened the door and she stepped in the limousine.

The driver closed the door, she pulled down the window and gave him some order in French…The sound of her voice was soft and yet cruelly sharp, it was a voice used to give orders and not to be contradicted.

Soon, there were eighteen bags of Harrods in the hands of the driver who took his loot from the boot of the limousine, eighteen dark green bags with the gold crown of Harrods, the most chic Department Stores of London.

Eighteen souls, is how many of them she had counted on the concrete floor of the Earl's Court Tube station, and now there were exactly eighteen bags in the hands of the driver.

The driver was pale and visibly upset. He whistled and the noise of that call felt like the call of a crow over a vulture.

One dirty man came out from the station, the others followed closely and the driver said:
"Hey you, come, something for you from the lady".

She watched from the window as he handed each bag after she gave him a nod, after she had approved personally each face and hand which took the Harrods bag from her driver,

It took but eighteen minutes, one minute per soul on a New Year morning in London, ten minutes.

Then the driver stepped back in the car and drove away, she did not close the window, the snow was entering the limousine, and it was a strange and very sad sight.

As the Earl Courts Station, the bums slowly went back to their corner, they opened their bags, each was filled with New Year gifts, foods and goodies, and there was too in each bag an envelope, full with a bunch of bank notes, each had been given 10,000 sterling pounds, shrieks of panic and joy and delirium were heard as the limousine pulled away quickly, some tried to run after the speeding car, to say thanks, some kneeled in the snow, praying to God…

The Limousine was speeding in the lonely and deserted streets of London, then it stopped by South Kensington, the porter of the mansion greeted the arrival of the limousine and then, the driver came out.

The lady told a few words in French to the driver and gave him a bag, a different bag and wished him a curt happy New Year…She stepped out of the back seat as the driver walked up the entrance of the building and she sat on the driver's seat She kicked off her high heels, and she informed in curt French that, she would drive around. As the limousine speeded back, a cry and sobs were heard from the Drayton Gardens Mansion, -South Kensington, the driver had open his bag and found

100,000 sterling pounds, tears rolled uncontrollably on his cheeks as he tried to run after her…. He tried to call her on his mobile, there were no connection…

The limousine speeded up steadily until it reached the Themes, then the polar bear limousine closed its eye lids, the motor stopped, she stepped out, and jumped in the icy waters of the polluted rover, drowning fast, she died in the lonely dream of a new year miracle of Earls Court 's poverty…

Her body was never found, the limousine was brought back to the mansion, her name never revealed. Some say she was an actress, some said she was an Arab, some said she was an Asian, some said she was a French poet, some called her anataalie, some Brigitte.None knew her, not even her driver….

It was New Year morning 2005.

ABOUT THE AUTHOR

Rahman,brigitte arlette is an award winning poet. French by birth, she spends her life travelling the world, living always in a new country. A chameleo, one would need chameleo words to properly describe her or her life.